CHESS OP

TRAP OF

THE DAY

About the Author

Life Master Bruce Alberston is a well-known teacher and trainer in New York. He's written and narrated the CD-Rom, *Quick Kills on the Chessboard* and is the author of *51 Chess Openings for Beginners*, and the bestselling *Chess Mazes*. For Cardoza Publishing, he and Fred Wilson have collaborated on *303 Tricky Chess Mates*, *303 Tricky Chess Tactics*, *303 Tricky Chess Puzzles*, *303 More Tricky Chess Puzzles*, *200 Capture Mates*, and *202 Checkmates for Children*.

CHESS OPENING TRAP OF THE DAY

Bruce Alberston

CARDOZA PUBLISHING

Cardoza Publishing is the foremost gaming publisher in the world, with a library of over 200 up-to-date and easy-to-read books and strategies. These authoritative works are written by the top experts in their fields and with more than 9,000,000 books in print, represent the best-selling and most popular gaming books anywhere.

FIRST EDITION

Copyright © 2007 by Bruce Alberston
- All Rights Reserved -

Library of Congress Catalog Card No: 2007933092
ISBN: 1-58042-217-9

Visit our web site—www.cardozapub.com—or write for a full list of books and computer strategies.

CARDOZA PUBLISHING
P.O. Box 1500, Cooper Station, New York, NY 10276
Phone (800) 577-WINS
email: cardozapub@aol.com
www.cardozapub.com

 # TABLE OF CONTENTS

# INTRODUCTION

The everyday opening mistakes made by amateurs often go both unnoticed and unpunished. In this book, I'll teach you how to notice *and* take advantage of these mistakes by setting opening traps. With these tactics, you'll be able to capture pieces and gain a decided advantage over your opponents—one you can take all the way to the final checkmate.

I'll show you how to use these traps in more than forty different openings. The tactical themes and basic guts of the trap tend to repeat over and over again, regardless of the opening selected. So when you learn to identify these patterns, you'll be able to easily spot the trap, the mistake which springs the trap, and the execution of moves you'll need to gain the advantage. You'll see where the loser went wrong, so you can improve your play from both sides of the opening.

This great collection of traps runs across a gamut of openings to give you an arsenal of weapons to win pieces and games. Armed with this powerful knowledge, you'll see an immediate improvement in your play. You'll also find yourself more often on the winning side of the game!

# SUGGESTIONS FOR IMPROVING YOUR PLAY

1. The king is not safe on his starting square in the center of the board. He's subject to all sorts of mating threats and tactical shots, particularly queen forks. The solution is to get the king out of the center by castling quickly. Get the kingside knight and bishop out and then castle. Don't just think about it, do it.

2. Beginners have a tendency to bring the queen out too early in the game, but this is wrong. The queen is a powerful piece that can come into the game any time you choose. There's no rush. Instead, concentrate on developing the knights and bishops, and getting castled. After the opening has settled down and the game has taken on a specific character, the queen is then in position to select her best working square. The flip side of bringing the queen out too early occurs after your opponent has made a mistake and fallen into your trap. How do you take advantage? Very often, it's with the queen. That's when you want to use the queen to inflict maximum punishment.

It's time to wind down the introductory remarks and let the *Chess Opening Trap of the Day* speak for themselves. Happy trapping!

SYMBOLS AND ABBREVIATIONS

K or ♔   stands for king
Q or ♕   stands for queen
R or ♖   stands for rook
B or ♗   stands for bishop
N or ♘   stands for knight
P or ♙   stands for pawn although in practice the "P" is rarely used.
0-0   stands for kingside castling
0-0-0   stands for queenside castling
†   stands for check
#   stands for mate or checkmate
1-0   White wins
0-1   Black wins

TRAP OF THE DAY:
Double King Pawn Openings

1. CENTER GAME

1.	e4	e5
2.	d4	d6

After this, White exchanges pawns, then the queens, and Black's king gets stuck in the center. It was better to take, 2...exd4.

3.	dxe5	dxe5
4.	Qxd8†	Kxd8
5.	Bc4	Ke8
6.	Nf3	Nd7
7.	Nc3	Ne7

The Black bishops are jammed in; that's White's signal to move against the king.

8.	Ng5	f6

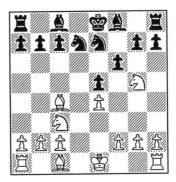

Saves his pawn but not the f7-square. It's mate in two.

9.	Bf7†	Kd8
10.	Ne6#	1-0

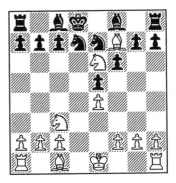

Black is checkmated.

11

2. CENTER GAME

1.	e4	e5
2.	d4	exd4
3.	Qxd4	d6

More energetic is 3...Nc6.

4.	Nc3	Be6
5.	Bb5†	Nd7
6.	e5	....

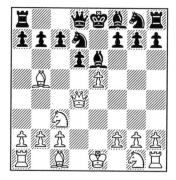

Premature. He should just bring out a new piece. Black can already play 6...c6, but he goes ....

6.	....	dxe5
7.	Qxe5	....

Overlooking the danger. First 7. Bxd7† and only then 8. Qxe5 was correct.

7.	....	c6

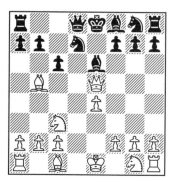

Breaks the pin on the knight. White's queen and bishop are now threatened. He has to lose one of them.

3. CENTER GAME

1. **e4** **e5**
2. **d4** ....

To open the center.

2. .... **exd4**
3. **Qxd4** ....

The one problem with the Center Game is that the queen has to come out early to insure recovery of the pawn. Black can gain time by attacking the queen with his knight.

3. .... **Nc6**

Sure enough Black attacks the queen, gaining time.

4. **Qc3** ....

A blunder; 4. Qe3 or 4. Qa4 were better squares.

4. .... **Bb4**

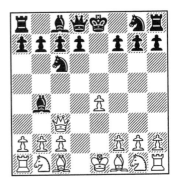

Black pins and wins the queen.

4. CENTER GAME

1.	e4	e5
2.	d4	exd4
3.	Qxd4	Nc6
4.	Qc4	....

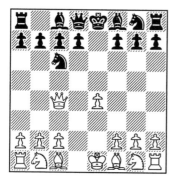

c4 is not a great square for the queen. She can be further attacked.

4.	....	Nf6
5.	f3	d5
6.	Qb3	Nd4
7.	Qc3	....

Better 7. Qd3. Now she's in trouble as Black combines bishop pin with knight fork to win the queen.

7.	....	Bb4
8.	Qxb4	Nxc2†
9.	Kd1	....

After 9...Nxb4 Black gains the queen for merely a bishop.

5. CENTER GAME

1.	e4	e5
2.	d4	exd4
3.	Qxd4	Nc6
4.	Qa4	Bc5

5.	Bc4	d6
6.	Bd5	Bd7
7.	Nf3	....

Safer 7. c3 so the queen can return to d1. Now the queen gets harassed by Black's knight and bishops.

7.	....	Nd4
8.	Qc4	Bb5

Black keeps attacking the queen. When she shifts to a dark square the other bishop goes into action.

9.	Qc3	Bb4
10.	Qxb4	....

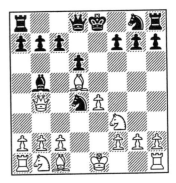

The follow up is 10...Nxc2† 11. Kd1 Nxb4.

6. DANISH GAMBIT

1.	e4	e5
2.	d4	exd4
3.	c3	dxc3
4.	Bc4	cxb2
5.	Bxb2	....

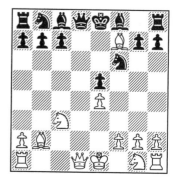

White sacrifices two pawns to get a big jump in development.

5.	....	d6
6.	Nc3	Nf6
7.	e5	dxe5

A slip. He should not have opened the d-line.

| 8. | Bxf7† | .... |

8.	....	Ke7
9.	Ba3†	Kxf7
10.	Qxd8	....

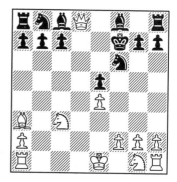

White has won queen for bishop. If 10...Bxa3 then 11. Qxh8 still leaves him way ahead in material.

7. IRREGULAR

1.	e4	e5
2.	Qh5	....

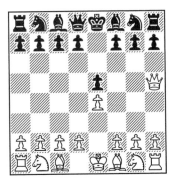

This "Terrorist Attack" is not a particularly good opening, but it works pretty well on beginners who don't know how to handle it. Very often they panic when they see an enemy queen in their half of the board.

2.	....	g6

A serious mistake. Black should guard his e5-pawn by 2...Nc6. In advancing the g-pawn, Black is thinking like a beginner.

He's hoping White won't see the attack on his queen and Black gets to take it. But of course, White does see it, and moves the queen with devastating effect.

3.	Qxe5†	....

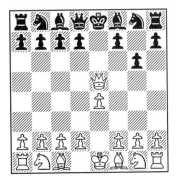

The queen takes the e5-pawn with check. It's also a fork. After Black blocks the check, White wins the rook in the corner, 4. Qxh8. That's the really dark side of Black's second move (2...g6). He opened the diagonal leading to the rook with his own hands.

8. IRREGULAR

1. e4	e5
2. Qh5	....

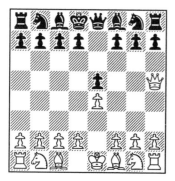

This "Terrorist Attack" works against beginners, but experienced players know how to deal with it.

2.	Ke7

The worst possible move that Black can make. There's a story behind it.

3. Qxe5# 1-0

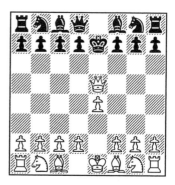

It happened at the Nationals. Black's king and queen were set up wrong, Kd8 and Qe8. Black saw the error and tried to correct it, but did not give advanced notice. So when he touched his king he was called for "touch move." He had to play the king and the only square was e7. You gotta' know the rules.

9. IRREGULAR

1.	e4	e5
2.	d3	Bb4†

5.	b4	Bb6
6.	a5	....

Useless. White just sticks a pawn in the bishop's face and Black has to retreat. He should have played 2... Bc5 or else brought out one of his knights.

3.	c3	Ba5
4.	a4	d5

Overlooking the effect of White's sly fourth move, Black doesn't see the danger to his bishop. Had he seen it he might have made an escape square by 4...a6 or 4...c6.

The Black bishop has been surrounded and trapped by the creeping White ants; I mean pawns. Black will lose his bishop for one of the pawns.

10. BISHOP'S OPENING

1.	e4	e5
2.	Bc4	....

The Bishop's Opening.

2.	....	Bc5
3.	c3	f6

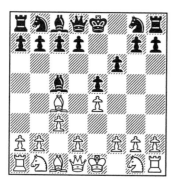

Exposes the king along the e8-h5 diagonal.

4. d4   exd4

The second error in a row. Two bad moves, back to back, is enough to lose the game. This one costs a piece because it opens up the fifth rank leading to the bishop.

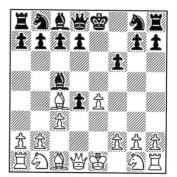

5. Qh5†   ....

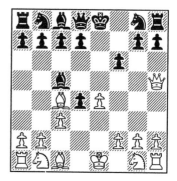

Exploiting the weakness of the e8-h5 diagonal. After 5...g6, there comes 6. Qxc5, picking off the undefended bishop. That leaves White ahead a bishop for a pawn.

20

11. BISHOP'S OPENING

1.	e4	e5
2.	Bc4	Bc5
3.	Qg4	....

Attacks the g7-pawn which Black guards with his king.

3.	....	Kf8

Not strictly defensive. It contains a drop of poison if White plays routinely.

4.	d3	....

Leaving the queen in line with the c8-bishop is a mistake. Here it is duly punished. 4. Qf3 was O.K.

4.	....	d5

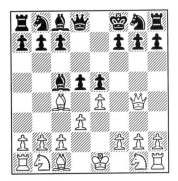

The d-pawn unmasks the c8-bishop while attacking c4. It's a double threat as White's queen and bishop are both attacked. He must lose one of them.

12. BISHOP'S OPENING

1.	e4	e5
2.	Bc4	Qh4

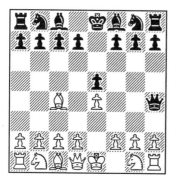

After White guards e4 the queen is misplaced.

3.	Nc3	Be7
4.	d3	h6
5.	Nd5	....

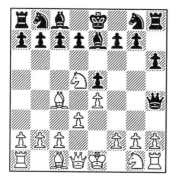

Excellent! The obvious threat is 6. Nxc7† forking king and rook. There's a hidden purpose as well.

5.	....	Bd8

Black guards c7 as expected.

6.	g3	....

The queen is lost. The knight denies her e7, f6, and there are no other safe squares to go to. This is the penalty for bringing the queen out too early.

13. BISHOP'S OPENING

1.	e4	e5
2.	Bc4	Nf6
3.	Nf3	Nxe4
4.	Nc3	Nxc3
5.	dxc3	....

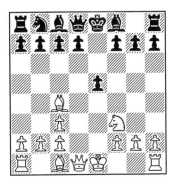

White sacrificed the e4-pawn to get a jump in development. His forces are ready to spring into action at a moment's notice.

5.	....	d6
6.	0-0	Bg4

A pin that doesn't pin. White moves his knight anyway, offering the queen.

7. Nxe5 ....

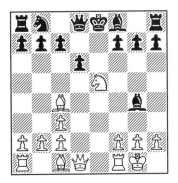

7.	....	Bxd1
8.	Bxf7†	Ke7
9.	Bg5#	1-0

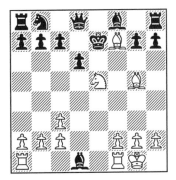

The Black king has been checkmated.

14. VIENNA GAME

1.	e4	e5
2.	Nc3	Nc6
3.	Bc4	d6
4.	Bd5	Qg5
5.	Bxc6†	bxc6
6.	d3	Qxg2

White should have guarded his g2-pawn. He didn't and now he has trouble guarding his rook.

7. Qf3 ....

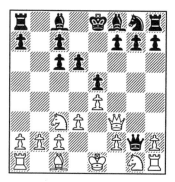

White comes up with his best defense. Black has to play cleverly if he wants to break it down.

7. .... Bh3

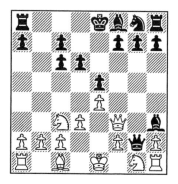

This does it. Black wins more material no matter how White replies. The basic threat is 8...Qxf3 9. Nxf3 Bg2 forking rook and knight.

If 8. Nxh3 then 8...Qxf3 gains the queen. And if 8. Qxh3, then 8...Qxh1 wins the exchange. Finally, there is 8. Ke2 Qf1† 9. Kd2 Bg2 forking queen and rook.

15. VIENNA GAME

1. e4	e5
2. Nc3	Nf6
3. Bc4	Nxe4

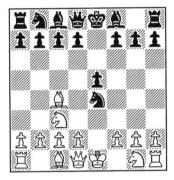

4. Bxf7†	Kxf7
5. Nxe4	d5
6. Qf3†	Kg8
7. Ng5	....

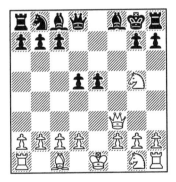

7.	Qxg5

Black takes the bait. 7...Qd7 would have defended everything.

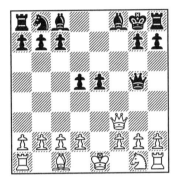

8. Qxd5†	Be6
9. Qxe6# 1-0	

Black is checkmated.

16. VIENNA GAME

1.	e4	e5
2.	Nc3	g6
3.	d4	d6
4.	dxe5	dxe5

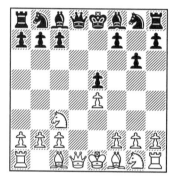

Trade queens or not? In fact the trade is in order as White gains developing time for his queenside pieces.

5.	Qxd8†	Kxd8
6.	Bg5†	f6
7.	0-0-0†	Ke8

The opening has not gone well for Black. White has several pieces out, Black has none. Plus the Black king, stuck in the middle, is a potential target. There should be something here for White.

8. Nd5 ....

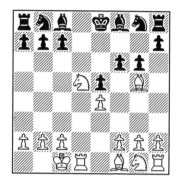

And so there is; a double attack by the White knight on the points c7 and f6. If Black takes the bishop, 8...fxg5, then White follows with 9. Nxc7† along with 10. Nxa8, winning the exchange. If Black defends by 8...Bd6, which is probably best, then White gains at least a pawn after 9. Nxf6† Nxf6 10. Bxf6.

26

17. VIENNA GAME

1. e4	e5
2. Nc3	Nf6
3. Bc4	Nc6

Bringing pieces out is what you're supposed to do.

4. d3	d6
5. Bg5	Be7

6.	Nxd5

Up to this point both sides have played well and the position is about even.

6. Nd5   ....

A slip. If he wants to go Nd5 he must first take the knight, 6. Bxf6.

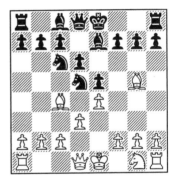

Wins material no matter how White recaptures: 7. Bxe7? Ndxe7 gains a full piece. Best is 7. exd5 Bxg5 8. dxc6 bxc6, when White is only one pawn behind.

18. KING'S GAMBIT

1.	e4	e5
2.	f4	....

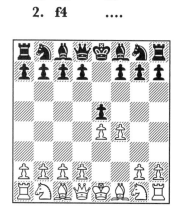

The King's Gambit, which Black may accept or decline. Here he declines.

2.	....	d6
3.	Nf3	Nc6
4.	Bc4	Be7
5.	fxe5	dxe5
6.	0-0	Nf6
7.	d3	Na5

The knight looks to trade off the c4-bishop. But who guards the e5-pawn? White thinks it can be taken for free. He's wrong.

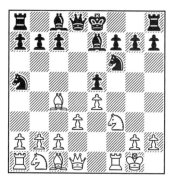

8.	Nxe5	....

The fatal capture.

8.	....	Qd4†

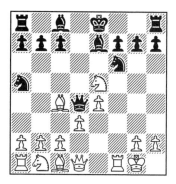

The queen forks both king and knight. White loses a piece.

19. KINGS GAMBIT

1.	e4	e5
2.	f4	Bc5

White offers his e4-pawn.

5.	....	Nxe4

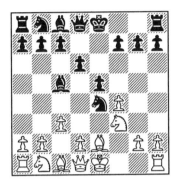

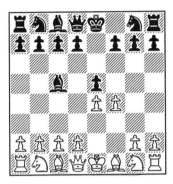

If 3. fxe5? Qh4†, White suffers after 4...Qxe4.

3.	Nf3	d6
4.	Be2	Nf6
5.	c3	....

Black takes the bait.

6.	Qa4†	....

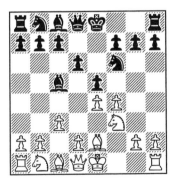

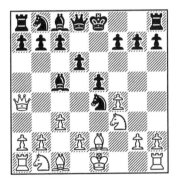

After 6...Nc6 7. Qxe4, White is up a piece.

29

20. KING'S GAMBIT

1.	e4	e5
2.	f4	d6
3.	Nf3	Bg4

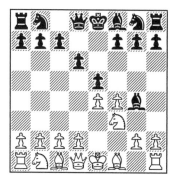

These kind of pins can easily backfire as the g4-bishop is not defended.

4.	Bc4	Be7

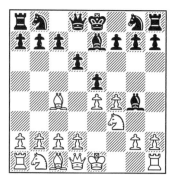

The correct move was 4...Nc6, putting another guard on his e5-pawn.

5.	fxe5	dxe5
6.	Bxf7†	....

A sacrifice to draw the king out and set up a knight fork.

6.	....	Kxf7
7.	Nxe5†	....

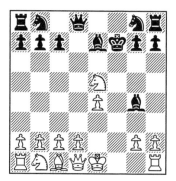

After Black saves his king, White recovers his piece by taking the bishop at g4. That puts him two pawns up.

21. KING'S GAMBIT

1.	e4	e5
2.	f4	Bc5
3.	fxe5	....

Black plays in classical style, developing his bishop while offering White his e5-pawn. White should not take the pawn. His best move was 3. Nf3, stopping Black's queen from giving check at h4.

3. .... Qh4†

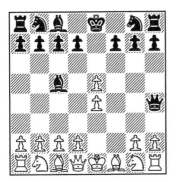

There is no good answer to the brutal queen check. If 4. g3 then 4...Qxe4† picks off the rook in the corner, 5...Qxh1. What happens now to White is even worse.

4. Ke2 ....

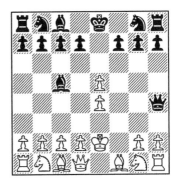

4. .... Qxe4#
0-1

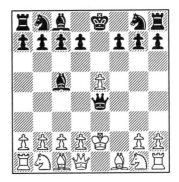

The White king has been checkmated.

22. KING'S GAMBIT

1. e4	e5
2. f4	d6
3. Nc3	Be6

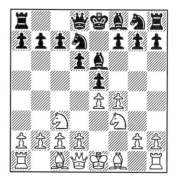

In the developing stage the short-stepping knights should get preference over the long-striding bishops.

4. Nf3   ....

Notice how White brings out his knights.

4. ....   Nd7

Black decides to bring out a knight, but he puts it on the wrong square. Better was 4...Nc6, guarding the e5-pawn, without jamming in the bishop.

5. f5   ....

The light-squared bishop is completely hemmed in and is lost. Black did this to himself.

23. KING'S GAMBIT

1.	e4	e5
2.	f4	d5
3.	exd5	e4

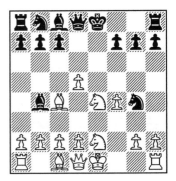

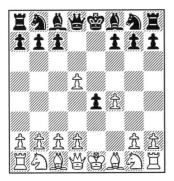

Black sacrifices a pawn to hamper White's development. The g1-knight cannot readily come out at f3.

4.	Bc4	Nf6
5.	Nc3	Bb4
6.	Nge2	....

A consequence of the pawn at e4, the knight comes out at e2, jamming the queen.

6.	....	Ng4
7.	Nxe4	....

White grabs the bait and pays the price. He had better: 7. d4 and 7. 0-0.

7.	....	Ne3

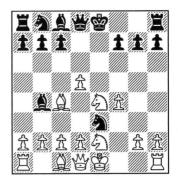

The queen is lost to the raiding knight as the d2-pawn is pinned.

24. KING'S GAMBIT

1.	e4	e5
2.	f4	exf4

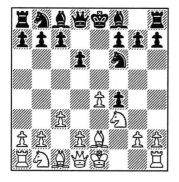

Black accepts the gambit. This part is okay.

3.	Be2	d6
4.	Nf3	Nf6
5.	c3	....

Black attacks the e4-pawn, but when White makes no obvious effort to defend it, Black should ask himself why. He doesn't.

5.	....	Nxe4

Black sees what looks like a free pawn, and without bothering to think, he grabs it. That's a no-no.

6.	Qa4†	....

Checks the king and attacks the e4-knight. Black ends up losing a knight for a pawn.

25. KING'S GAMBIT

1.	e4	e5
2.	f4	exf4
3.	Nf3	d5

A good active defense, breaking up White's center.

4.	exd5	Nf6
5.	Bb5†	c6
6.	dxc6	Nxc6
7.	0-0	....

Both sides appear to have things in order, but this natural move upsets the balance. It's a mistake due to the weakening of the a7-g1 diagonal brought about by White second move, f2-f4.

Instead of castling he should play either 7. d4 or else 7. Bxc6†.

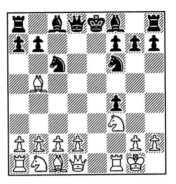

7.	....	Qb6†

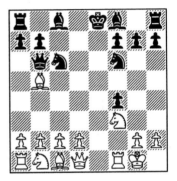

The queen check picks off the undefended bishop, or the knight if 8. Nd4.

26. KING'S GAMBIT

1.	e4	e5
2.	f4	exf4
3.	Nf3	d5
4.	Nc3	....

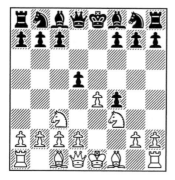

It was simpler to just take the pawn, 4. exd5. But White gets cute. He'll let Black take first.

4.	....	dxe4
5.	Nxe4	Bg4
6.	Qe2	....

Queen opposite the king is usually a danger signal. Does Black pick it up?

6.	....	Bxf3

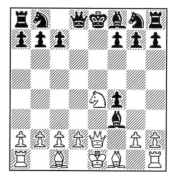

A huge mistake, no doubt expecting recapture on f3. He had to block, 6...Be7.

7.	Nf6#	1-0

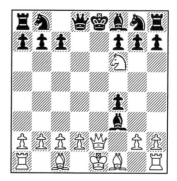

Double check and mate. Game over just like that.

27. KING'S GAMBIT

1.	e4	e5
2.	f4	exf4
3.	Bc4	Qh4†
4.	Kf1	b5
5.	Bxb5	Nf6
6.	Qf3	g5

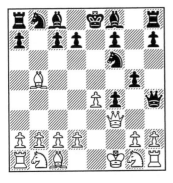

7.	e5	Ng4
8.	g3	Nxh2†

The play is fast and loose, typical for the King's Gambit.

9.	Rxh2	Qxh2

Momentarily, White has an extra knight, but Black's next move threatens mate.

10. Qxa8 ....

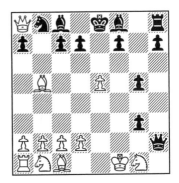

10.	....	fxg3
11.	Qg2	Bb7

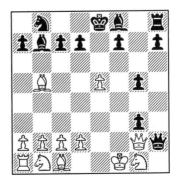

12. Qxb7 Qf2#; 12. Qxh2 gxh2 and promotes. On 12. Nf3 Qxg2† 13. Kxg2 g4 recovers the piece. And if 12. Qe2 g2† 13. Kf2 Bc5† It's all very messy.

28. KING'S GAMBIT

1.	e4	e5
2.	f4	exf4
3.	d3	Qh4†

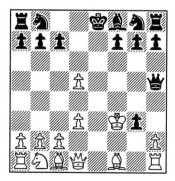

White's third move was weak; there is now no comfortable answer to the queen check.

4.	Ke2	d5
5.	exd5	Bg4†
6.	Nf3	Bxf3†
7.	Kxf3	Qh5†

The *en passant* pawn capture re-opens the line leading to White's queen.

Skewering king and queen. White attempts a diagonal block with his g-pawn.

9.	Kxg3	Qxd1

| 8. | g4 | .... |

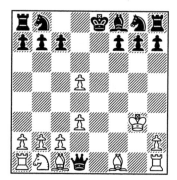

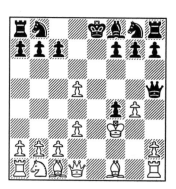

Black has won a queen for nothing.

| 8. | .... | fxg3† |

38

29. KING'S GAMBIT

1.	e4	e5
2.	f4	exf4
3.	Nf3	g5
4.	Bc4	f6

A better way to secure the g5-pawn is by 4...Bg7 and 5...h6. His fourth move only weakens the e8-h5 diagonal. White can now sacrifice his knight with impunity, opening a path for his queen to reach h5.

5. Nxg5 ....

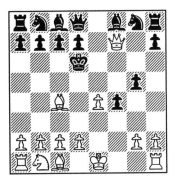

White drives the king out, then he drives him back.

8.	Qd5†	Ke7
9.	Qe5#	1-0

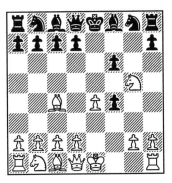

5.	....	fxg5
6.	Qh5†	Ke7
7.	Qf7†	Kd6

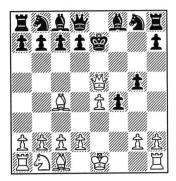

The king has been hunted down and checkmated.

30. KING PAWN GAME

1.	e4	e5
2.	Nf3	h6

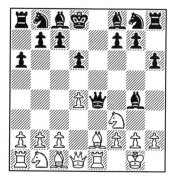

9. Bb5 ....

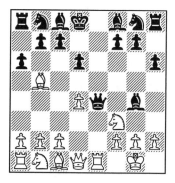

Weak. Technically it doesn't lose a pawn, but it takes too much time and energy to get the pawn back.

3.	Nxe5	Qe7
4.	d4	d6
5.	Nf3	Qxe4†
6.	Be2	Bg4
7.	0-0	Kd8

King and queen on the same line is trouble. So the king moves off.

8.	Re1	a6

8...a6 was designed to stop Bb5. But it doesn't do the job. White plays it anyway. If 9...Qf5 10. Re8# So, he has to give up his queen for rook and bishop: 9...Qxe1† 10. Qxe1 axb5.

31. DAMIANO DEFENSE

analysis: after 13. Qxh7†

1.	e4	e5
2.	Nf3	f6
3.	Nxe5	fxe5
4.	Qh5†	g6
5.	Qxe5†	Qe7
6.	Qxh8	Nf6
7.	d3	d5
8.	Bg5	Nbd7

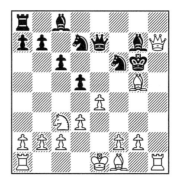

He doesn't do that.

9.	Bxf6	Nxf6
10.	f3	Kf7
11.	Nd2	Bg7

Black's opening is tricky but inferior and so far White has done everything right. But he has to know how to extricate his queen from the corner. The best way is 9. Nc3 c6 10. h4 Kf7 11. h5 and the queen gets out after 11...Bg7 12. hxg6† Kxg6 13. Qxh7† etc.

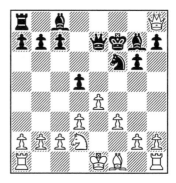

The White queen is trapped and lost.

32. DAMIANO DEFENSE

1.	e4	e5
2.	Nf3	f6
3.	Nxe5	Qe7

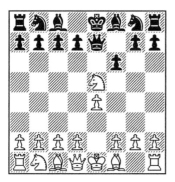

Better than taking the knight, 3...fxe5? 4. Qh5†, etc. Plus it sets a trap: 4. Qh5† g6 5. Nxg6 Qxe4† and 6...Qxg6. White makes the correct reply and Black still has to tread carefully.

4.	Nf3	Qxe4†
5.	Be2	Nc6
6.	Nc3	Qg6
7.	0-0	Ne5

Black steps onto a landmine. It was better to shift the queen to a safer square, 7...Qf7. Even then Black's position does not inspire confidence.

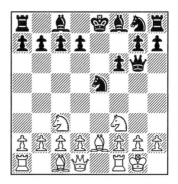

8.	Nxe5	fxe5
9.	Bh5	....

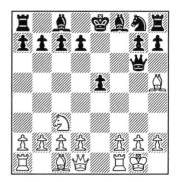

White pins and wins the Black queen.

33. LATVIAN GAMBIT

1. e4	e5
2. Nf3	f5

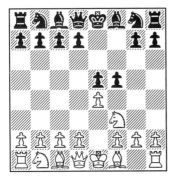

This is the Latvian Counter Gambit, a violent attempt to steal the initiative. It's generally considered unsound.

3. Nxe5	Qf6
4. d4	d6
5. Nc4	fxe4
6. Be2	Be7
7. Nc3	Qg6

When the Latvian can be made to work, Black gets his queen on g6 and his knight to f6. White's sixth move (Be2) is designed to prevent this from happening. Apparently Black did not take notice. A just punishment follows.

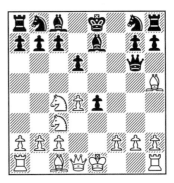

8. Bh5	....

White wins the queen by pinning against the king.

34. PHILIDOR DEFENSE

1.	e4	e5
2.	Nf3	d6

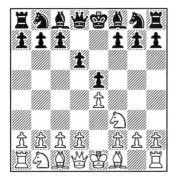

Philidor's Defense, putting a solid guard on the e5-pawn, another pawn.

3.	c3	Bg4
4.	d4	Nf6
5.	dxe5	Nxe4

Probably Black thinks he's keeping the pawns even, but in fact there's more than just a pawn at stake. What he has to do is get rid of White's f3-knight so he can recapture on e5: 5...Bxf3 6. Qxf3 dxe5. That does keep the pawns even.

6.	Qa4†	....

Followed up by 7. Qxe4 winning a full knight. You gotta' watch out for those slimy queen forks when your king is still on his starting square.

35. PHILIDOR DEFENSE

1. e4	e5
2. Nf3	d6
3. Bc4	Bg4
4. Nc3	g6

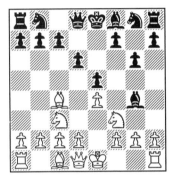

Better to bring out a knight. The pawn move gives White a chance for a "brilliancy."

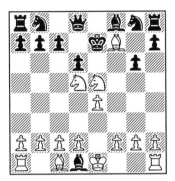

The Black king has been checkmated. The mating pattern with bishop and two knights, plus the set up queen sacrifice was first played by the French Master Legal in his game against St. Brie (1750's). They are both dead now and so is Black's king. But Legal's Trap lives on for two and a half centuries, catching many unwary queen-nabbbers.

5. Nxe5 ....

Offering the queen. Black could cut his losses by taking the knight, 5...dxe5 6. Qxg4. But the queen is so tempting.

5.	Bxd1
6. Bxf7†	Ke7
7. Nd5#	1-0

36. PHILIDOR DEFENSE

1.	e4	e5
2.	Nf3	d6
3.	d4	Nd7
4.	Bc4	Nb6
5.	Bb3	exd4
6.	Qxd4	Qf6
7.	Qd3	Bg4
8.	Bg5	Qxb2

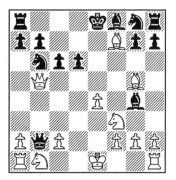

A good response to White's last move is 8...Qg6. But Black notices the newly undefended b2-pawn and figures that it's safe to take it. The reason why it's not safe is cleverly hidden.

9.	Qb5†	c6
10.	Bxf7†	....

10.	....	Kxf7
11.	Qxb2	....

White has won the enemy queen for just one bishop. Once the Black queen stepped onto the b2-square everything was forced. The checks did the job.

46

37. PHILIDOR DEFENSE

1. e4	e5
2. Nf3	d6
3. Bc4	Nd7
4. d3	a6

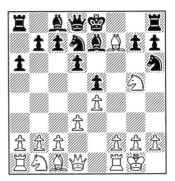

If he wants to move one of the queenside pawns, 4...c6 makes more sense. It controls d5 and gives the Black queen some air.

5. Ng5	Nh6
6. 0-0	Be7

Jams the queen up even more. Better ...c6, or ...Qe7

7. Bxf7†	....

Opens e6 for the knight.

7.	Nxf7
8. Ne6	....

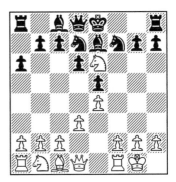

The queen suffocates. She has no escape from the knight attack.

38. PHILIDOR DEFENSE

1.	e4	e5
2.	Nf3	d6
3.	Bc4	Be7
4.	Nc3	Nd7
5.	d4	Ngf6
6.	0-0	0-0
7.	h3	c6

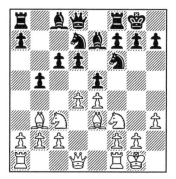

The bishop had to retreat to d3.

9. .... b4

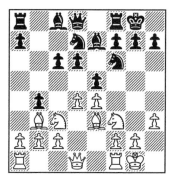

After the c3-knight moves, Black wins an important center pawn for free, 10...Nxe4.

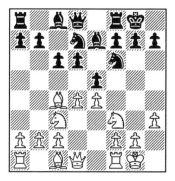

Good play by both sides up to this point. But here White is advised to play the restraining move, 8. a4, to stop Black from expanding on the queenside.

8.	Be3	b5
9.	Bb3	....

39. PHILIDOR DEFENSE

1.	e4	e5
2.	Nf3	d6
3.	d4	Nd7
4.	c3	Ne7

Playing the king-knight to e7 jams Black up. The most natural placement for the knight was 4...Ng8-f6.

5.	dxe5	dxe5
6.	Bc4	h6

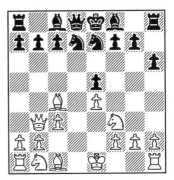

Black can't stop the invasion at f7. About the only thing we can see is 7...Nc5, but then comes 8. Bxf7† Kd7 9. Nxe5† Kd6 10. Qd1† and Black is quite lost.

analysis: after 10. Qd1†

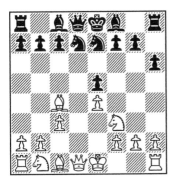

To stop 7. Ng5, but after Black's mistake on move four, it's not easy to give good advice.

| 7. | Qb3 | .... |

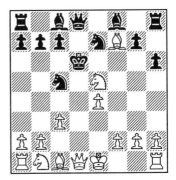

40. PHILIDOR DEFENSE

1.	e4	e5
2.	Nf3	d6
3.	d4	Qf6

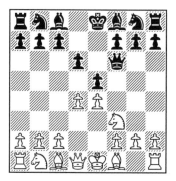

Using the queen to defend e5 is inefficient. He should find another, cheaper way.

4.	Nc3	Be6

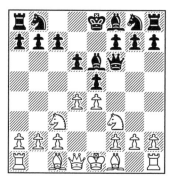

5.	dxe5	dxe5

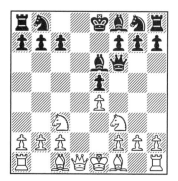

Better to move the queen than recapture.

6.	Bg5	....

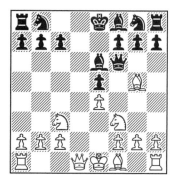

If Black saves his queen, 6...Qg6, he gets mated, 7. Qd8#. So the queen is lost.

41. PHILIDOR DEFENSE

1.	e4	e5
2.	Nf3	d6
3.	d4	Bg4
4.	dxe5	Bxf3
5.	Qxf3	dxe5
6.	Bc4	Nf6
7.	Qb3	....

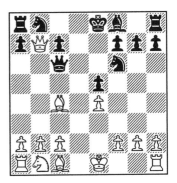

To guard the rook.

9. Bb5 ....

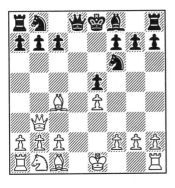

7. .... Qd7

Black's string of second rate moves add up to one big mistake. He had to stop 8. Bxf7† Kd7 9. Qe6# But 7...Qe7 was the better way. True, 8. Qxb7 loses a pawn, but after 8...Qb4† he's out of any immediate danger.

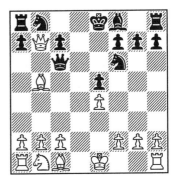

Trying to save his rook, Black loses his queen to a bishop pin.

8. Qxb7 Qc6

42. PETROFF DEFENSE

1.	e4	e5
2.	Nf3	Nf6
3.	Nxe5	Nxe4

The essence of the Petroff is counterattack on the e4-pawn. But the way to get the pawn back is by 3...d6 4. Nf3 and only then 4... Nxe4.

4. Qe2 ....

4. .... Nf6

Black overlooks the enemy threat. His only chance was 4...Qe7 5. Qxe4 d6. That gets his piece back, but he loses a pawn.

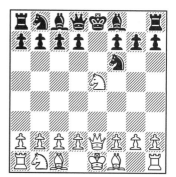

5. Nc6† ....

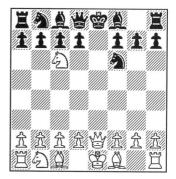

A direct attack on Black's queen and a discovered attack (check) on Black's king. After saving the king he loses the queen. This is one of the standard traps that everyone has to know.

43. PETROFF DEFENSE

1.	e4	e5
2.	Nf3	Nf6
3.	Nxe5	Nc6

Black offers a gambit to speed his development. Strictly speaking, the gambit is not correct.

4.	Nxc6	dxc6
5.	d3	Bc5
6.	Bg5	....

7.	Bxd8	Bxf2†
8.	Ke2	Bg4#
	0-1	

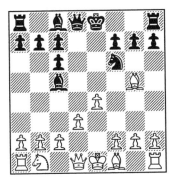

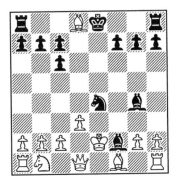

The right way was 6. Be2 followed by castling. Then White has a safe game with an extra pawn.

6.	....	Nxe4

This is yet another version of Legal's famous queen sacrifice followed by mate. See Trap #35 for the original setting.

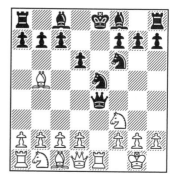

44. PETROFF DEFENSE

1.	e4	e5
2.	Nf3	Nf6
3.	Nxe5	Qe7

A complicated way of getting his pawn back. The simple way, 3...d6 4. Nf3 Nxe4, was the best way.

4.	Nf3	Qxe4†
5.	Be2	d6
6.	0-0	Nc6
7.	Re1	Ne5

The right way to block off the e-file was by 7...Be7. Trying to do it with the knight, leaves Black wide open for a shot.

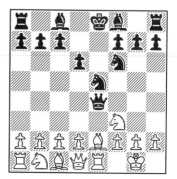

8. Bb5† ....

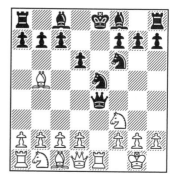

Check to the king and discovered attack on the queen. After 8...c6 9. Rxe4 Nxe4, Black loses his queen for a rook.

45. PETROFF DEFENSE

1.	e4	e5
2.	Nf3	Nf6
3.	d4	....

A good alternative to 3. Nxe5. But when Black takes on d4, White should follow up with 4. e5.

3.	....	exd4
4.	Bd3	h6

A useless pawn move which is better replaced by 4...Nc6. Now White comes back to right idea.

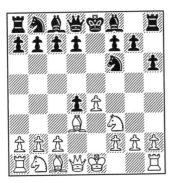

5.	e5	Ng4

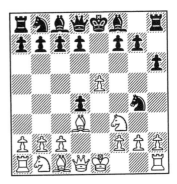

Sloppy play culminates in an outright mistake. The knight should play to d5.

6.	h3	....

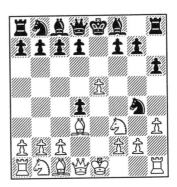

Black can get two pawns for the knight, but two pawns really isn't enough.

55

46. SCOTCH GAMBIT

1.	e4	e5
2.	Nf3	Nc6
3.	d4	exd4
4.	c3	....

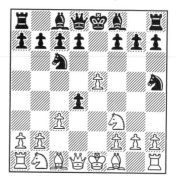

4. ....   Nf6

Black could take 4...dxc3. Declining as Black does here, is often the safer option. Not necessarily better, just safer.

6. g4   ....

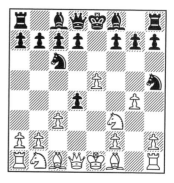

5. e5   Nh5

The knight should head for the center. Either 5...Nd5 or 5...Ne4 were playable. Veering off to the side of the board invariably leads to trouble.

The knight is lost, hung out to dry on the edge of the board.

47. SCOTCH GAMBIT

1. **e4**	**e5**
2. **Nf3**	**Nc6**
3. **d4**	**exd4**
4. **c3**	**d6**

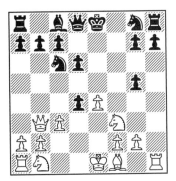

Better to push the d-pawn two squares, 4...d5. After the text, White can simply play 5. cxd4 with some advantage. But he gets carried away. Ultimately, however, his imagination is rewarded.

5. **Bg5**	**Be7**
6. **h4**	**Bxg5**
7. **hxg5**	**f6**
8. **Qb3**	**fxg5**

Black overlooks the enemy threat. That happens often.

9. **Rxh7**	**Rxh7**
10. **Qxg8†**	**....**

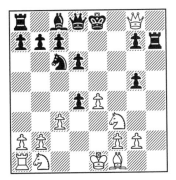

Followed by 11. Qxh7, regaining the rook and emerging a piece ahead.

48. SCOTCH GAME

1.	e4	e5
2.	Nf3	Nc6
3.	d4	d6
4.	Nc3	Nge7

An awkward, self-blocking move which allows White a strong attack, even after trading queens.

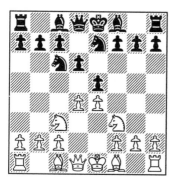

5.	dxe5	dxe5
6.	Qxd8†	Kxd8
7.	Ng5	Ke8
8.	Bc4	Nd8
9.	Nb5	Bd7

The pressure of constantly defending takes it's toll and Black blunders. He had to lose something, but it didn't have to be his king.

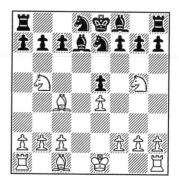

10. Nxc7# 1-0

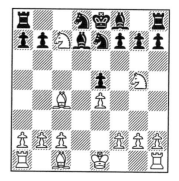

Black is checkmated with his king on his starting square: Smothered mate by the knight.

49. SCOTCH GAME

1.	e4	e5
2.	Nf3	Nc6
3.	d4	exd4
4.	Nxd4	Bc5
5.	Be3	Nf6

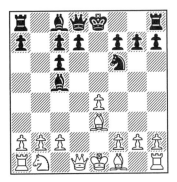

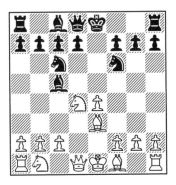

Black plays out a routine developing move, which does not take notice that White's last move (Be3) was suitable for both defense and attack. A good safe move for Black is 5...Bb6. Also good, but somewhat more complicated is 5...Qf6, keeping up the pressure on the d4-knight.

6. Nxc6   bxc6

7. Bxc5   ....

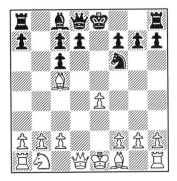

White's unmasking tactic, a discovered attack, has worked. The enemy bishop has been won for practically nothing.

50. SCOTCH GAME

1.	e4	e5
2.	Nf3	Nc6
3.	d4	exd4
4.	Nxd4	Nf6
5.	f3	Bc5
6.	Nb3	Bb6
7.	Bb5	0-0
8.	a4	Nxe4

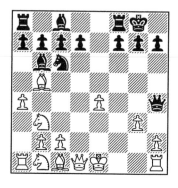

10.	....	Qxe4†
11.	Kd2	Qe3#
	0-1	

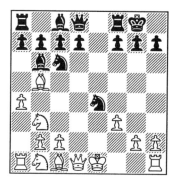

Aggression usually pays even if not 100% sound. Here, White's uncastled king provides the motive.

9.	fxe4	Qh4†
10.	g3	....

White is in trouble no matter what he does. Best may be 10. Kd2.

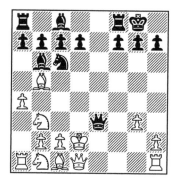

White is duly checkmated. At the end, White had to lose something; unfortunately, it was his king.

51. SCOTCH GAME

1.	e4	e5
2.	Nf3	Nc6
3.	d4	exd4
4.	Nxd4	....

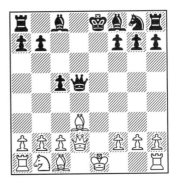

4. .... Nxd4

Gives White the upper hand in the center. Better to play 4...Nf6 or 4...Bc5.

5.	Qxd4	c5
6.	Qd2	d6
7.	Bd3	d5

Black tries to recover ground in the middle. But the whole operation has a huge tactical flaw.

8. exd5 Qxd5

Black still doesn't see what's wrong. He had to let the pawn go.

9. Bb5† ....

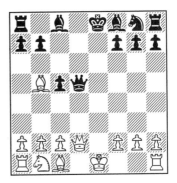

And 10. Qxd5 wins the Black queen.

52. SCOTCH GAME

1.	e4	e5
2.	Nf3	Nc6
3.	d4	exd4
4.	Nxd4	Qh4

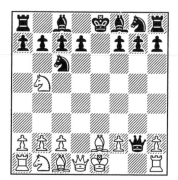

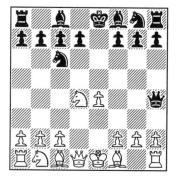

These early excursions by the queen rarely turn out well against accurate play. Here White can attack the c7-square which the queen left undefended.

5.	Nb5	Qxe4†
6.	Be2	Qxg2

There's nothing better now than 6...Kd8. When he takes at g2, Black gets two threats to worry about, the old one at c7, and the new one at g2.

7. Bf3 ....

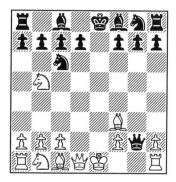

After the queen moves, White continues 8. Nxc7† and takes the rook at a8.

53. SCOTCH GAME

1.	e4	e5
2.	Nf3	Nc6
3.	d4	exd4
4.	Nxd4	Qh4

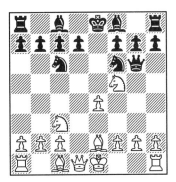

It's hard to recommend this early queen move. Even if it turns out to be playable, Black has to be super careful that the queen does not get lost.

5.	Nc3	Nf6
6.	Nf5	Qh5

8. Nh4 ....

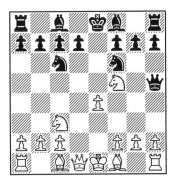

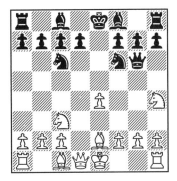

The queen runs from the knight, but picks the wrong square. She had to try 6...Qg4 and hope.

Black's queen is attacked and there's no way out. White has all the escape squares covered.

7.	Be2	Qg6

54. THREE KNIGHTS

1.	e4	e5
2.	Nf3	Nc6
3.	Nc3	g6
4.	d4	exd4
5.	Nd5	Bg7
6.	Bg5	Nge7

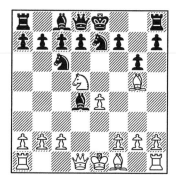

Not expecting White's next.

8.	Qxd4	Nxd4
9.	Nf6†	Kf8
10.	Bh6#	1-0

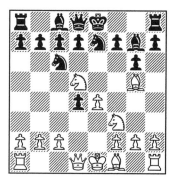

Better 6...Nc6-e7, leaving the g8-knight to cover the dark squares f6 and h6.

7. Nxd4 ....

Threatens 8. Nxc6 and 9. Bxe7, so the knight has to be removed. Since 7...Nxd4 fails to 8. Bxe7, he must take with the bishop, but then he gets a surprise.

7. .... Bxd4

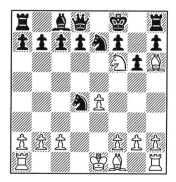

Black has been mated.

55. THREE KNIGHTS

1.	e4	e5
2.	Nf3	Nc6
3.	Nc3	d6
4.	Bc4	h6
5.	d4	Bg4
6.	dxe5	Nxe5

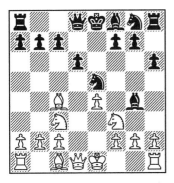

8.	Bxf7†	Ke7
9.	Nd5#	1-0

Black figures this is okay because the f3-knight is pinned. In fact it loses by force. He had to take back with the d6-pawn.

7. Nxe5   Bxd1

Slightly better is 7...dxe5 8. Qxg4 which loses only the bishop. Now White has mate in two moves.

Black has fallen into Legal's mate. It's one of the neatest ways to win a chess game. Everyone should do it at least once.

56. FOUR KNIGHTS

1.	e4	e5
2.	Nf3	Nc6
3.	Nc3	Nf6

Guess why this is called the Four Knights Game?

4.	Bb5	Nd4
5.	Nxd4	exd4
6.	Ne2	c5

Apparently played to guard the d4-pawn, but there's a more insidious motive at work. Suppose White now puts a solid guard on his e4-pawn?

7. d3 ....

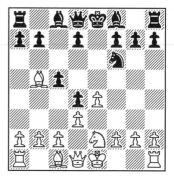

Which is what he does. Instead he had to guard the pawn by 7. Ng3.

7. .... Qa5†

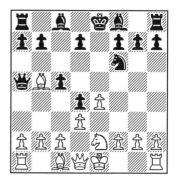

White gets out of check and Black gets the b5-bishop.

57. FOUR KNIGHTS

1.	e4	e5
2.	Nf3	Nc6
3.	Nc3	Nc6
4.	Bb5	d6
5.	0-0	Qd7

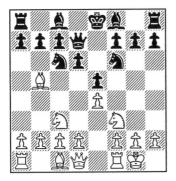

If Black truly wants to break the pin on the c6-knight, then he should go 5...Bd7.

6. Nd5   Nxd5

Black captures the wrong unit. The undefended e4-pawn was the thing to take, 6...Nxe4. Now White is able to pile up on the pinned knight.

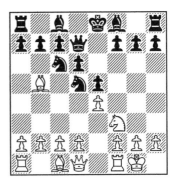

7.	exd5	a6
8.	dxc6	....

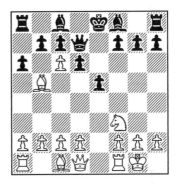

Black's queen is attacked, so he has no time to take the White bishop. After 8...bxc6, the bishop withdraws and White is ahead a piece for a pawn.

58. ITALIAN GAME

1.	e4	e5
2.	Nf3	Nc6
3.	Bc4	f6
4.	d4	Na5

The attack on the bishop causes Black more pain than it does White. The bishop has an easy way out. The knight doesn't.

5.	Bxg8	Rxg8
6.	dxe5	fxe5

He has to let the pawn go and bring his knight back to civilization by 6...Nc6. Recapturing makes things worse.

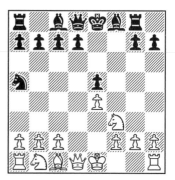

7.	Qd5	Rh8
8.	Qxa5	....

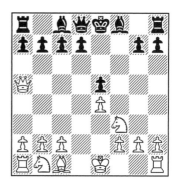

White has won a knight for nothing. That's often the penalty for placing a knight on the edge of the board, especially on a square that is undefended.

59. ITALIAN GAME

1. e4	e5
2. Nf3	Nc6
3. Bc4	Nd4

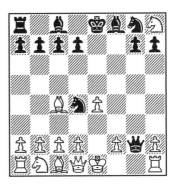

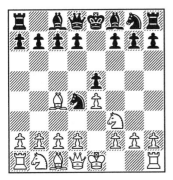

Black plays a move of no strategic merit whatsoever. All it does is serve up one of the nastiest traps in the book. If White is alert he plays 4. Nxd4 with the better game. If he's not alert, well, you'll see what happens.

4. Nxe5	Qg5
5. Nxf7	Qxg2
6. Nxh8	....

If 6. Rf1 Qxe4† 7. Be2 Nf3#.

6.	Qxh1†
7. Bf1	Qxe4†
8. Be2	Nxc2†
9. Kf1	Qh1#
	0-1

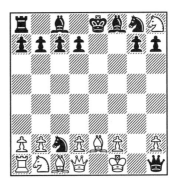

At the end it was mate or loss of the queen.

60. GIUOCO PIANO

1.	e4	e5
2.	Nf3	Nc6
3.	Bc4	Bc5
4.	Nc3	d6
5.	d3	Bg4

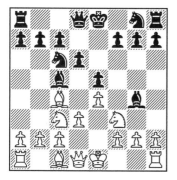

So far, so good. But now White begins a faulty combination.

6.	Bxf7†	Kxf7
7.	Ng5†	....

No doubt White was figuring on 7...king-moves, 8. Qxg4. No doubt he's overlooked Black's next idea.

7.	....	Qxg5

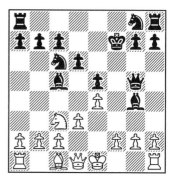

8. Bxg5   Bxd1

After 9. Rxd1 you can see that Black is one piece ahead. He's taken three, White only two. The pawn captured at f7, doesn't weigh in the balance. It's just the officers.

61. RUY LOPEZ

1.	e4	e5
2.	Nf3	Nc6
3.	Bb5	Nf6
4.	d3	Ne7

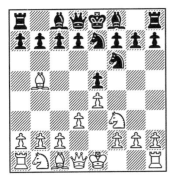

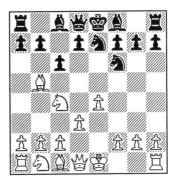

6.	....	cxb5
7.	Nd6#	1-0

This baits a trap which White does best to ignore.

5. Nxe5   c6

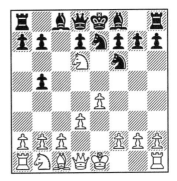

Attacks the bishop, and if the bishop retreats, 6. Bc4, then 6... Qa5† forks king and knight. In desperation, White sets a trap of his own. It works when Black gets impatient.

Black's king has been checkmated. He should not have captured the bishop. Instead, 6...Ng6 7. Ba4 b5, would have won a piece.

6. Nc4   ....

62. RUY LOPEZ

1.	e4	e5
2.	Nf3	Nc6
3.	Bb5	d6
4.	Nc3	g6

Intending ...Bg7, but he doesn't follow up.

5.	d4	exd4
6.	Nd5	....

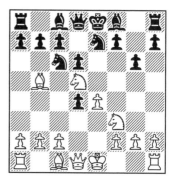

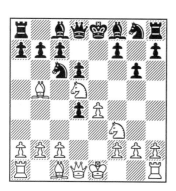

The simple recapture, 6. Nxd4, was good, but White wants to confuse the issue.

6.	....	Nge7

And he succeeds. Black is confused and does not recognize the danger. He should play 6...Bg7, to keep a guard over the sensitive f6-square.

7.	Nf6#	1-0

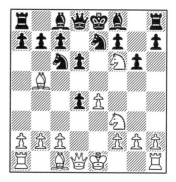

The weakness of f6 is telling. Black has fallen into checkmate.

63. RUY LOPEZ

1.	e4	e5
2.	Nf3	Nc6
3.	Bb5	d6
4.	d4	Bd7
5.	Nc3	Nge7
6.	Bc4	exd4
7.	Nxd4	g6
8.	Bg5	Bg7
9.	Nd5	....

10.	....	0-0

Black castles, hoping it will turn out better than 10...Nxd4 11. Nf6† Kf8 12. Bh6 mate. It doesn't.

11.	Nf6†	Kh8
12.	Ng4†	Nxd4
13.	Bf6†	Kg8
14.	Nh6#	1-0

Black is in trouble. White wants to win the pinned e7-knight by removing the guard, 10. Nxc6, followed by 11. Bxe7. Black tries to counter by taking off the d4-knight, but White has a brilliant reply.

9.	....	Bxd4
10.	Qxd4	....

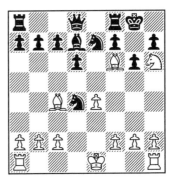

Black has been checkmated.

64. RUY LOPEZ

1.	e4	e5
2.	Nf3	Nc6
3.	Bb5	a6
4.	Bxc6	dxc6

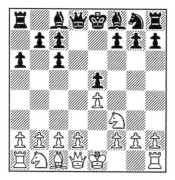

Now 5. Nxe5 doesn't win a pawn because of 5...Qd4 6. Nf3 Qxe4† and Black gets the pawn back.

5.	0-0	f6
6.	d4	exd4
7.	Nxd4	Bc5

If he wants to attack the knight, a better way is by 7...c5. The problem with the bishop move is that nothing guards the bishop when it comes to c5.

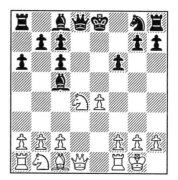

| 8. | Qh5† | .... |

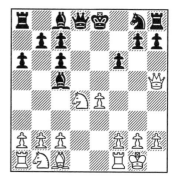

Double attack (a fork) on the king and bishop. After Black saves his king, 8...g6, White collects the bishop, 9. Qxc5.

74

65. RUY LOPEZ

1.	e4	e5
2.	Nf3	Nc6
3.	Bb5	a6
4.	Ba4	Nge7
5.	d3	b5
6.	Bb3	....

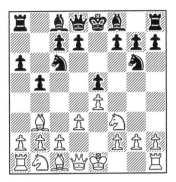

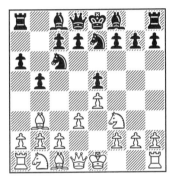

Combining defense and attack. White saves his bishop and lines up against the sensitive f7-square.

6. .... Ng6

Black does not see the danger. He has to play 6...h6 to stop White's knight from coming in.

7. Ng5 ....

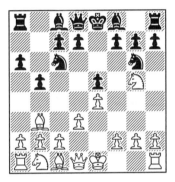

There is no way to keep White out of f7. He's going to win at least a pawn. If 7...f6, then 8. Nf7 forks queen and rook, winning the exchange.

66. RUY LOPEZ

1.	e4	e5
2.	Nf3	Nc6
3.	Bb5	a6
4.	Ba4	d6
5.	d4	b5
6.	Bb3	Nxd4
7.	Nxd4	exd4

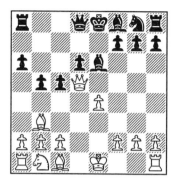

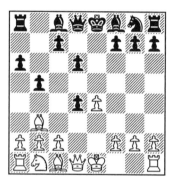

8. Qxd4 ....

This natural recapture is a mistake. He should play first 8. Bd5 or else, 8. c3, turning the opening into a gambit.

8.	....	c5
9.	Qd5	Be6

10.	Qc6†	Bd7
11.	Qd5	c4

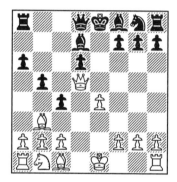

White's threats are at an end, and he must lose his b3-bishop, which is surrounded by Black's pawns. This is the famous Noah's Ark Trap.

76

67. RUY LOPEZ

1.	e4	e5
2.	Nf3	Nc6
3.	Bb5	a6
4.	Ba4	d6
5.	Bxc6†	bxc6
6.	d4	d6
7.	Nc3	Rb8

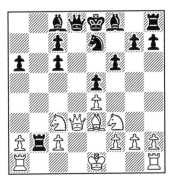

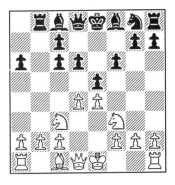

11.	Qxd8†	Kxd8
12.	0-0-0†	....

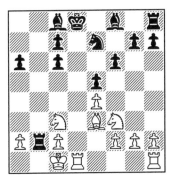

This last move, attacking b2, is to discourage White from moving his c1-bishop. It turns out that White can move the bishop anyway.

8.	Qd3	Ne7
9.	Be3	Rxb2
10.	dxe5	dxe5

Black has fallen into the trap. White confiscates the rook with an unusual form of double attack.

After Black saves his king, White takes at b2.

68. RUY LOPEZ

1.	e4	e5
2.	Nf3	Nc6
3.	Bb5	a6
4.	Ba4	Nf6

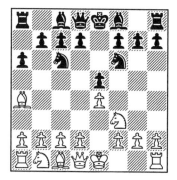

Attacks the e4-pawn.

5.	d3	Be7

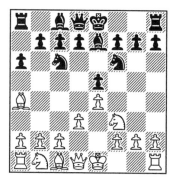

A careless move; Black is not alert. He should try to protect his own e5-pawn by 5...d6.

6.	Bxc6	dxc6
7.	Nxe5	....

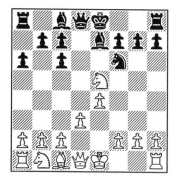

White has won an important center pawn for nothing; 7...Qd4 doesn't work because of the simple 8. Nf3. In fact, there is no way for Black to get the pawn back. The whole idea of the Ruy Lopez is to put pressure on the Black e5-pawn, looking to win it if Black gets careless, as he does here.

TRAP OF THE DAY:
Asymmetrical King Pawn Openings

69. OWEN'S DEFENSE

1.	e4	b6
2.	Nc3	Ba6
3.	Bxa6	Nxa6
4.	Qe2	Qc8
5.	Nd5	Nf6

6.	....	Qxa6
7.	Nxc7†	Kd8
8.	Nxa6	....

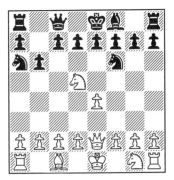

White's last move contained a threat which Black fails to notice. He should withdraw his a6-knight back to b8. Then he's safe.

6. Qxa6 ....

Black's queen turns out to be overloaded, unable to guard both a6 and c7. That's what makes White's combination click.

White wins a piece. The attempt to trap the knight by 8...e6 9. d3 Kc8 fails after 10. a3 Kb7 11. Nb4, when the knight reaches safety.

70. OWEN'S DEFENSE

1.	e4	b6
2.	d4	Bb7
3.	Bd3	f5
4.	exf5	Bxg2

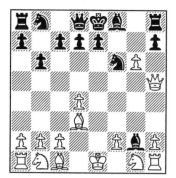

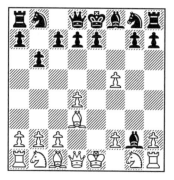

At first glance it appears that White has been suckered into losing his rook. But it's a case of the trapper being trapped. White now opens fire on Black's king.

5.	Qh5†	g6
6.	fxg6	Nf6

Attacking White's queen looks good, but it doesn't work. The best chance was 6...Bg7, creating an escape square for the king at f8.

7.	gxh7†	Nxh5
8.	Bg6#	1-0

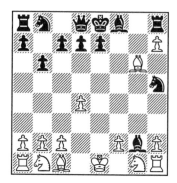

Black has been done in along the Fool's Mate diagonal, e8-h5.

71. CENTER COUNTER

1. e4	d5
2. exd5	Qxd5
3. d4	b6

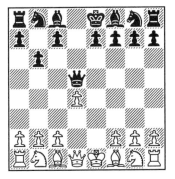

The c8-bishop can easily come out along the c8-h3 diagonal. So there's no reason to make a new diagonal for the bishop. A good line for Black is 3...Nc6 4. Nf3 Bg4.

4. Be2   Qxg2

White baits the trap and Black's greed gets the best of him. He thinks he's winning a rook. In fact he's losing a rook.

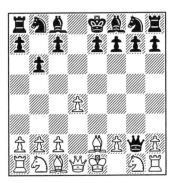

5. Bf3   ....

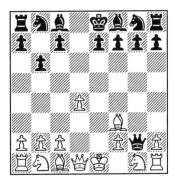

Black's queen and rook are forked. After Black moves his queen away, 5...Qg6, White takes the rook in the corner, 6. Bxa8, gaining a rook for a pawn.

72. CENTER COUNTER

1.	e4	d5
2.	exd5	Qxd5
3.	d4	Nc6
4.	Nf3	Bg4
5.	Be2	Bxf3

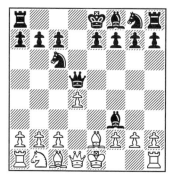

Black has a good game, but it is better to hold off on this trade. The reason Black makes it is that he thinks he can win the d4-pawn by getting rid of the defending knight.

6. Bxf3   Qxd4

Consistently following his plan. This is a good idea when the plan is good. But when the plan is bad, it's best to veer off. That's what Black should do here.

7. Bxc6† bxc6

First White knocks out the prop from under Black's queen. Then he takes the queen for nothing, 8. Qxd4.

73. CENTER COUNTER

1. e4   d5

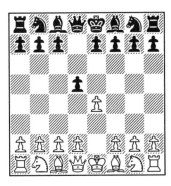

The characteristic move of the Center Counter, which is nothing more than an attack on the e4-pawn.

2. exd5   Qxd5
3. Ke2   ....

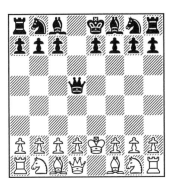

White got called for "touch move." White touched his king and had to move it. The only square the king can go to is e2. It's the worst possible move that White can make, but there was no choice.

3. ....   Qe4#

0-1

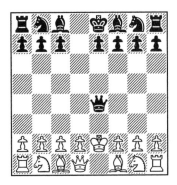

Say "I adjust" beforehand and you don't get called for "touch move." I know. I've used this story before and I'll probably use it again because it bears repeating.

74. CENTER COUNTER

1.	e4	d5
2.	exd5	Qxd5

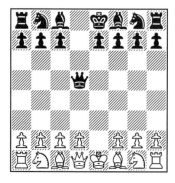

The Center Counter is a good defense for Black. But there is one downside. In order to recover the lost pawn, Black's queen gets sucked out into the center of the board very early. When the queen gets attacked, it's not so clear where she's supposed to go.

3. Nc3   Qc6

Black's queen got attacked and she's picked the wrong square to run to. There were three better squares: a5, d6, and safest of all, d8.

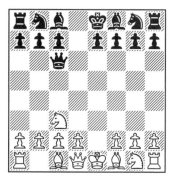

4. Bb5   ....

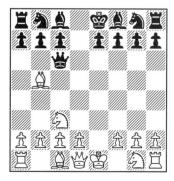

The Black queen is pinned and lost. Black can get a bishop for the queen, but it's really not enough.

75. ALEKHINE DEFENSE

1. e4	Nf6
2. e5	Ne4

The knight is supposed to go to d5 when attacked by the e-pawn. It looks like Black is playing an opening he doesn't really know. That can be dangerous.

3. b4	Nc6

Black's last knight move is just too casual. White was threatening something and Black doesn't see what it is. He should have played 3...e6, attacking the b4-pawn with his bishop.

4. d3	....

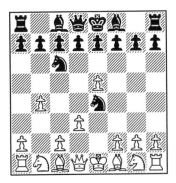

The attacked knight has no where to go. It's trapped. Black can get two pawns for the knight by 4... Nxf2 5. Kxf2 Nxe5. But the extra piece should prove stronger than the two pawns.

76. ALEKHINE DEFENSE

1.	e4	Nf6
2.	e5	Nd5

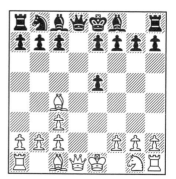

6. Bxf7† ....

This is certainly better than 2... Ne4. Still, Black must be on his guard since the knight can be further attacked, even on d5.

3.	Nc3	Nxc3
4.	dxc3	d6
5.	Bc4	dxe5

Attacking the e5-pawn on the previous move was okay. But taking the pawn is not okay, at least not in this position. The reason is that White has a bishop sacrifice to deflect Black's king away from the queen.

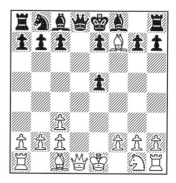

After the forced 6...Kxf7 White comes away with the queen, 7. Qxd8. Queen for bishop and pawn is a good deal. Take it when you can.

77. ALEKHINE DEFENSE

1. e4	Nf6
2. e5	Nd5
3. d4	Nc6

This doesn't look quite right. Black should go after the e5-pawn with a pawn, 3...d7-d6. That gives White more of a problem to solve. The way the game goes, White is able to tee off against the d5-knight.

4. c4	Nb6
5. Nc3	g6

White's strategy is directed against the b6-knight, but Black doesn't see what's coming. He should have moved one of his center pawns, either the d-pawn or the e-pawn.

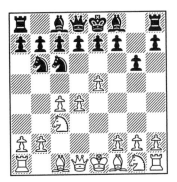

6. c5	....

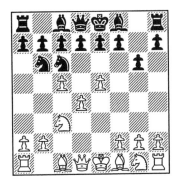

Check out the squares and you see that the b6-knight has nowhere to go.

78. ALEKHINE DEFENSE

1.	e4	Nf6
2.	e5	Nd5
3.	d4	g6
4.	c4	Nb6
5.	Be2	d6
6.	exd6	....

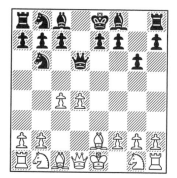

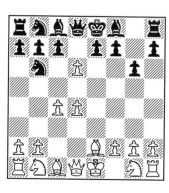

6. ....   Qxd6

7. c5   ....

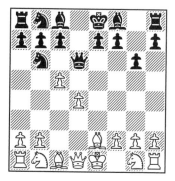

Of the three ways to recapture on d6, Black selects the one way which is definitely wrong. No doubt Black was thinking of developing a new piece, but in bringing out the queen he runs right into a pawn fork. He should have taken back with one of his pawns, maybe the c-pawn.

The pawn attacks both queen and knight. Naturally, Black will save his queen, but that means he loses his knight. Advantage White.

79. PIRC DEFENSE

1. e4	d6
2. Nf3	....

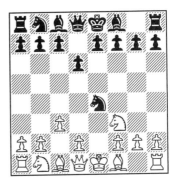

2. d4 is normal but there's nothing wrong with bringing out the king-knight.

2.	Nf6
3. c3	....

4. Qa4† ....

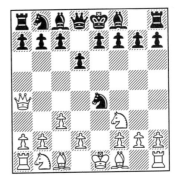

Instead of guarding his e4-pawn directly, White guards it indirectly. In other words he sets a trap.

The queen picks off the knight. White wins a piece.

3. .... Nxe4

Black thinks he's winning a pawn for nothing. That's not the case. Instead, he should continue in Pirc style with 3...g6, 4...Bg7, and 5...0-0.

80. PIRC DEFENSE

1.	e4	d6
2.	d4	Nf6
3.	Nc3	g6
4.	Nd5	....

We can't recommend this move. It's only purpose is to set Black up for a fall.

4. .... Nxe4

Black takes the bait. This part is okay. It's the next move that counts.

5. Qe2 ....

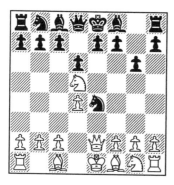

After 5...c6 6. Qxe4 cxd5 7. Qxd5, Black is in decent shape. He can continue with 7...Bg7 and 8...0-0.

5. .... Nf6

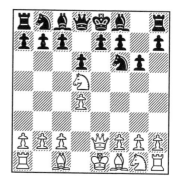

Black doesn't see it.

6. Nxf6# 1-0

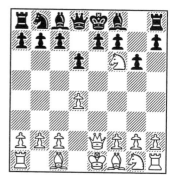

Black is checkmated.

81. CARO-KANN

1.	e4	c6
2.	d4	d5
3.	e5	Bf5
4.	Ne2	h6
5.	Ng3	Bh7
6.	c4	dxc4
7.	Bxc4	Nd7

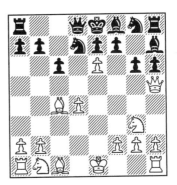

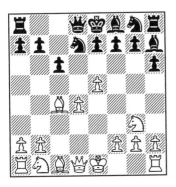

9.	....	gxh5
10.	exf7#	1-0

Safest was 7...e7-e6 and then 8... Nd7. Now 8. e5-e6 causes trouble but White figures to do even better.

8.	Qh5	g6
9.	e6	....

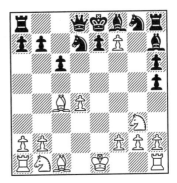

Checkmate. I hate being checkmated by a pawn.

Black has to take something with a pawn He should make the capture on e6, but instead he takes the queen. Too bad.

82. CARO-KANN

1.	e4	c6
2.	d4	d5
3.	e5	Bf5
4.	Ne2	h6
5.	Ng3	Bh7
6.	c3	Nd7

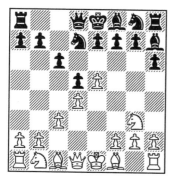

Too soon. He should play the e-pawn up one square. Now White makes a very promising sacrifice to break up the Black pawns.

7.	e6	fxe6
8.	Qh5†	g6
9.	Be2	....

Offering up the queen which Black must decline.

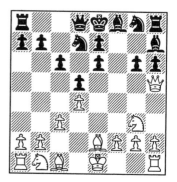

9.	....	gxh5

Any other move is better.

10.	Bxh5†	Bg6
11.	Bxg6#	1-0

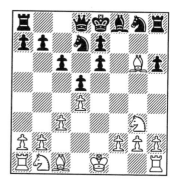

Mated along the Fool's Mate diagonal, e8-h5.

83. CARO-KANN

1.	e4	c6
2.	d4	d5
3.	Nc3	e6

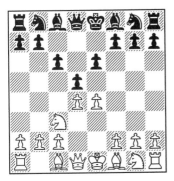

This last move leads to a cramped position. Better to trade 3...d5xe4 and get some freedom.

4.	Nf3	Bd7
5.	Bf4	Na6
6.	Qd3	Qe7
7.	0-0-0	0-0-0

Black's previous three moves were designed to set up for queen-side castling. Now he does it, but it's all wrong.

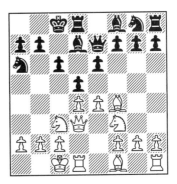

8. Qxa6 bxa6

Otherwise he's just a piece down. But taking is worse.

9. Bxa6# 1-0

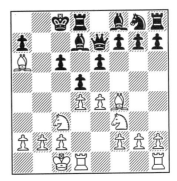

The criss-cross mate with the two bishops.

84. CARO-KANN

1.	e4	c6
2.	d4	d5
3.	Nc3	dxe4
4.	Nxe4	Nf6

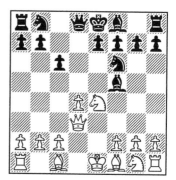

An early treatment of the Caro-Kann, still okay. Today 4...Nd7 or 4...Bf5 are more often seen.

5. Qd3 ....

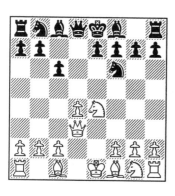

6.	Nxf6†	exf6
7.	Qxf5	...

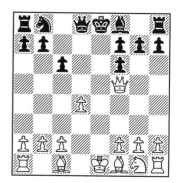

5. .... Bf5

White has won a bishop.

Apparently pinning the e4-knight. Pins by undefended bishops easily backfire as the opponent turns them into discoveries. That's the case here. Black should swap knights: 5...Nxe4 6. Qxe4. Then 6...Qd5, and a trade of queens, leaves him with a good game.

85. SICILIAN DEFENSE

1.	e4	c5
2.	b4	....

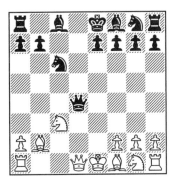

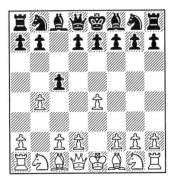

8.	Nd5	Qxb2
9.	Nxc7#	1-0

The Sicilian Wing Gambit. It may not be completely sound, but it leads to interesting play.

2.	....	cxb4
3.	Bb2	Nc6
4.	d4	d5
5.	exd5	Qxd5
6.	c4	bxc3
7.	Nxc3	Qxd4

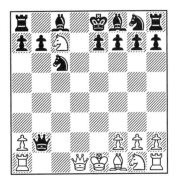

The second player has been checkmated.

Taking the pawn seems most natural, but Black has overlooked White's spectacular reply. Best was to withdraw the queen to d8, but even then, White looks to have strong compensation.

86. SICILIAN DEFENSE

1.	e4	c5
2.	c3	e6
3.	d4	Nf6
4.	e5	Nd5
5.	Nf3	f5
6.	Be2	Nc6

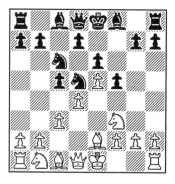

When a White pawn shows up at d4 Black is supposed to take, ...c5xd4. That's the main idea of the Sicilian Defense. Here, Black puts it off till it's too late. Now the White pawns rush forward causing havoc.

7.	c4	Nb6
8.	d5	Ne7

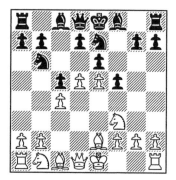

Black tries to dodge the oncoming pawns, but he can't. They keep coming.

9.	d6	Nc6
10.	Bg5	....

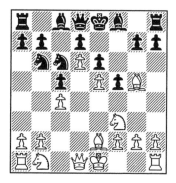

Black has to jettison a piece to save his queen.

87. SICILIAN DEFENSE

1.	e4	c5
2.	c3	d5
3.	exd5	Qxd5
4.	d4	cxd4
5.	cxd4	Nc6
6.	Nf3	Nf6
7.	Nc3	Qa5
8.	d5	Nb4
9.	a3	Nbxd5

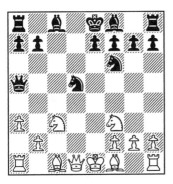

A clash of ideas. Black thinks the d5-pawn is weak and he takes it. White knows better and sets out to prove it. First the Black king is drawn to the d-file, setting up a pin, so the knight can't move.

10.	Bb5†	Bd7
11.	Bxd7†	Kxd7

Then the Black queen is driven away.

12. b4 ....

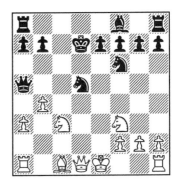

After 12...Qb6 13. Nxd5, White wins a knight.

88. SICILIAN DEFENSE

1.	e4	c5
2.	Nc3	d6
3.	f4	g6
4.	d4	Nf6

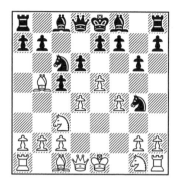

Black is afraid to take, 4...cxd4 because 5. Qxd4 hits the rook in the corner. Still, 5...Nf6 is a sufficient defense. Not taking at d4 lands Black in trouble.

5. e5   Ng4

On g4 the knight gets hung up to dry. The safer move was 5...Nf6-d7.

6. Bb5†   Nc6

If 6...Bd7, then 7. Qxg4.

7.	d5	a6
8.	dxc6	axb5
9.	cxb7	Bxb7
10.	Qxg4	....

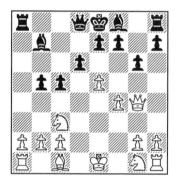

White has won a piece.

89. SICILIAN DEFENSE

1. e4   c5
2. d4   cxd4
3. Qxd4   Qa5†

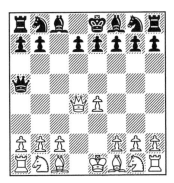

Best is 3...Nc6. Bringing the queen out early doesn't help Black's cause.

4. Bd2   Qh5
5. Nf3   d6
6. Na3   Nc6
7. Bb5   Nf6
8. 0-0-0   g6

Too slow. Better 8...Bd7.

9. e5   dxe5

Black is already in trouble, and opening the d-file makes things worse. White sacs the queen, gives a double check, then mates.

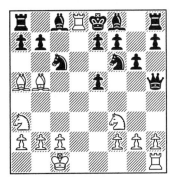

10. Qd8†   Kxd8
11. Ba5†   Ke8
12. Rd8#   1-0

Black is checkmated.

90. SICILIAN DEFENSE

1.	e4	c5
2.	Nf3	Nf6

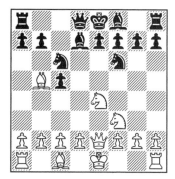

Attacks the e4-pawn. White could push, 3. e4-e5, but he prefers to play it safe, guarding the pawn.

3.	Nc3	d5
4.	Bb5†	Bd7
5.	Qe2	dxe4

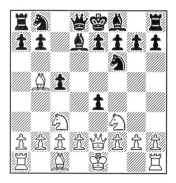

Black makes the correct decision. Trading on e4 relieves much of the pressure. But on the next move he fails to follow through, and that's where he makes his mistake.

6.	Nxe4	Nc6

Overlooking the threat. He should remove the knight, 6...Nxe4; then he's okay.

7.	Nd6#	1-0

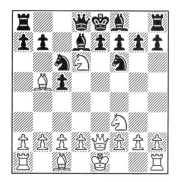

A pin mate. The e7-pawn can't take the knight.

100

91. SICILIAN DEFENSE

1.	e4	c5
2.	Nf3	Nf6
3.	e5	Nd5
4.	Bc4	Nb6
5.	Bxf7†	Kxf7

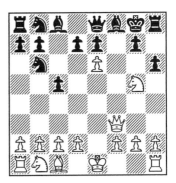

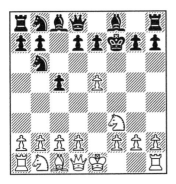

9.	Qf7†	Qxf7
10.	exf7#	1-0

The sacrifice can't be right. True, the Black king is exposed to future attacks, but that just means he has to be careful.

6.	Ng5†	Kg8
7.	Qf3	Qe8
8.	e6	h6

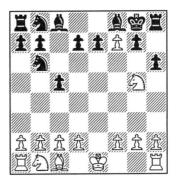

Checkmate by a pawn.

White does his best to stir up trouble, and succeeds. Black now panics and tries to drive away the knight. Instead, the calm 8...dxe6 was called for. Then he's in good shape.

92. SICILIAN DEFENSE

1.	e4	c5
2.	Nf3	Nc6
3.	d4	cxd4
4.	Nxd4	e6

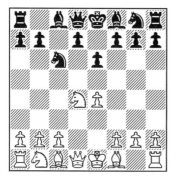

Black curls up into a tight little ball and defies White to get at him.

5.	Nc3	a6
6.	g3	Nge7
7.	Nb3	d6
8.	Bg2	Bd7
9.	Qxd6	....

The d6-pawn looks like a freebie, so without much thinking, White takes it off. He should have looked a little bit harder. Then he might have spotted...

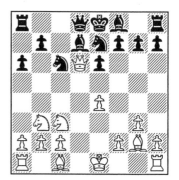

9.	....	Nd5

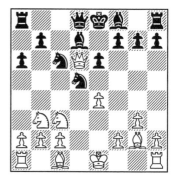

The queen is trapped. He could try 10. exd5 Bxd6 11. dxc6, but two minor pieces are not enough to make up for a lost queen.

93. SICILIAN DEFENSE

1. e4   c5
2. Nf3   d6
3. Ng5

This move can't be good. But even a weak move can become strong if you let down your guard.

3. ....   Qc7
4. Bb5†   Kd8

When I was starting out, I was told that the only way to get out of check was to move the king. I didn't learn about blocking the check until later. Of course, that's what Black should do here, block the check.

4...Bd7, 4...Nd7, and 4...Nc6 were all good ways.

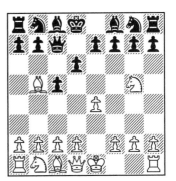

5. Nxf7# 1-0

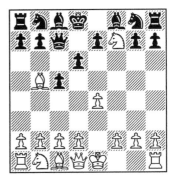

Black is checkmated. The weak White third move turned out to be strong in the end. But only because Black let it happen.

94. SICILIAN DEFENSE

1.	e4	c5
2.	Nf3	d6
3.	c3	Nc6

These days the preference is for 3...Nf6. The b8-knight can stay at home for a move or two.

4.	d4	Nf6
5.	Be2	Nxe4

Black reckons that the capture is safe since White has no queen check at a4. But watch what happens after the c6-knight gets pushed out of position by the advancing d-pawn.

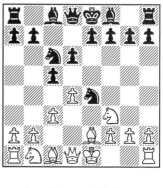

6.	d5	Ne5

The knight must move and when it does, the magical queen check appears.

7. Qa4† ....

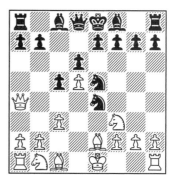

Fork on e8 and e4.

95. SICILIAN DEFENSE

1. e4	c5
2. Nf3	d6
3. d4	cxd4
4. Qxd4	Nc6
5. Bb5	Nf6

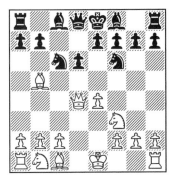

Best is to address the pin right away, 5...Bd7.

6. Bg5	h6
7. Bd2	g6
8. 0-0	Bg7
9. Rd1	Nh5

And here castling was in order. By leaving his king in the center Black makes problems for himself.

10. e5	dxe5

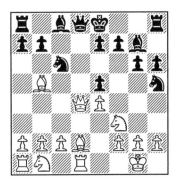

11. Qxd8†	Kxd8
12. Ba5†	Ke8
13. Rd8#	1-0

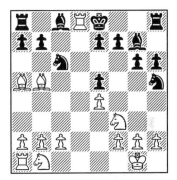

The Black king has been checkmated.

96. SICILIAN DEFENSE

1. e4	c5
2. Nf3	d6
3. d4	cxd4
4. Nxd4	Nf6
5. Nc3	a6

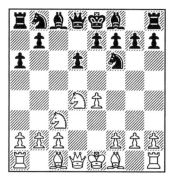

Najdorf's Variation, where the play can go off in many directions. After White's next move, Black decides to target the b2-pawn. It's very risky business.

6. Bg5	e6
7. f4	Qb6
8. a3	Qxb2

Blindly following his plan. Black should first play 8...Bd7. Then he really does threaten the b2-pawn.

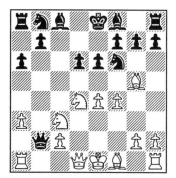

9. Na4	....

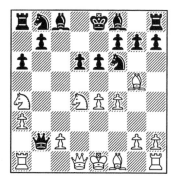

The queen is trapped. The best she can do is take the rook, but it's not enough to make up for the lost queen.

97. FRENCH DEFENSE

1. e4 e6
2. d4 Qh4

Early queen raid; not a good idea. Normal is 2...d5.

3. Bd3 h5
4. Nf3 Qg4

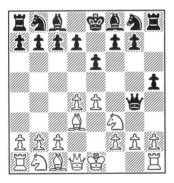

The queen has lingered too long on the kingside. She had to drop back, preferably to d8.

5. h3 ....

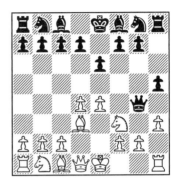

Black will be lucky if he can save his queen. Here are some typical variations.

(A) 5...Qxg2 6. Rg1 Qxh3 7. Bf1
(B) 5...Qg6 6. e5 Qxg2 7. Rh2
(C) 5...Qg6 7. e5 f5 8. exf6 Qxf6
9. Bg5 Qf7 10. Ne5
(D) 5...Qg6 7. e5 f5 8. exf6 Qf7
9. Ne5 Qxf6 10. Bg6† Ke7 (10...
Kd8 11. Bg5) 11. h4 with 12.
Bg5.

98. FRENCH DEFENSE

1. e4   e6
2. d4   d5

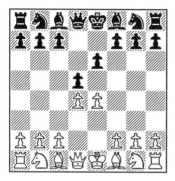

The standard starting position for the French Defense. White's e4-pawn is attacked and there are various things he can do about it.

3. Bd3   dxe4
4. Bxe4   Nf6
5. Bd3   ....

The bishop could also drop back to f3. But White prefers to bait a little trap.

5. ....   Qxd4

Black bites. The right way to get rid of White's d4-pawn is with another pawn: 5...c7-c5.

6. Bb5†   ....

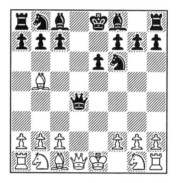

Check with discovery on the queen. If 6...Nc6 7. Qxd4 still wins the queen.

99. FRENCH DEFENSE

1. e4	e6
2. d4	d5
3. exd5	exd5

The Exchange Variation.

4. Nf3	Bg4
5. Qe2†	Be7

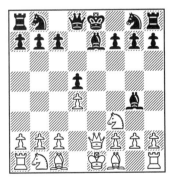

Blocking with the bishop drops a pawn. Safest is 5...Qe7, pinning White's queen.

6. Qb5† ....

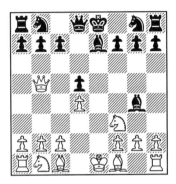

Attacks the king, the b7-pawn, and the d5-pawn. Depending on how Black gets out check, one of the two pawns is lost. Actually, this is a borderline trap. In order to win a pawn, White must lose time with his queen. So Black gets some compensation. Still nothing is clear, so we'll go for the pawn.

100. FRENCH DEFENSE

1.	e4	e6
2.	d4	d5
3.	e5	c5

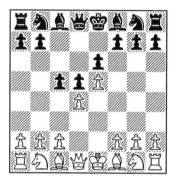

The Advance Variation.

4.	Qg4	cxd4
5.	Nf3	f5
6.	Qg3	Nc6
7.	Be2	Bd7
8.	Nxd4	Nxd4

This is wrong. Maybe Black can try the crazy idea 8...Bb4† 9. c3 Nxd4 when 10. Bh5† is met by 10... Kf8. White can vary with 10. Qxg7, but it's another game.

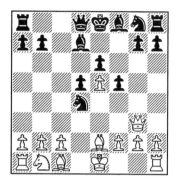

9.	Bh5†	Ke7

Or 9...g6 10. Bxg6† hxg6 11. Qxg6† and mates shortly with the c1-bishop.

10.	Qa3#	1-0

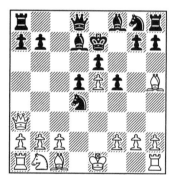

A criss-cross checkmate.

101. FRENCH DEFENSE

1.	e4	e6
2.	d4	d5
3.	Nd2	....

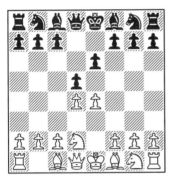

This is designed to avoid the pinning variation, 3. Nc3 Bb4.

3.	....	c5
4.	exd5	exd5
5.	dxc5	Bxc5
6.	Nb3	Bd6

Of course the bishop can also withdraw to b6. Dropping back to d6 sets a trap. Maybe White will take the d5-pawn.

7.	Qxd5	....

The pawn is tainted.

7.	....	Bb4†

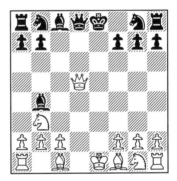

Check to the king and discovery on the queen. White loses the queen.

102. FRENCH DEFENSE

1. e4	e6
2. d4	d5
3. Nd2	c5
4. dxc5	Bxc5
5. Qg4	Nf6

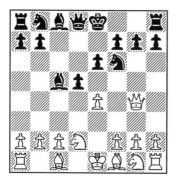

Black has no reason to fear the capture on g7. He has everything under control. White's early queen raid is going to backfire.

6. Qxg7	Rg8
7. Qh6	Bxf2†
8. Kxf2	....

White has to move his king (d1 or e2). Taking the bishop is much worse. It allows a knight fork.

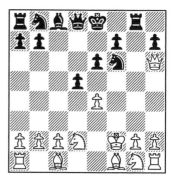

8. ....   Ng4†

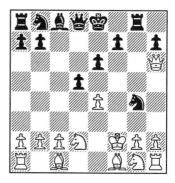

After White saves his king, Black removes the queen. That leaves Black ahead a queen for a bishop.

103. FRENCH DEFENSE

1.	e4	e6
2.	d4	d5
3.	Nc3	c5

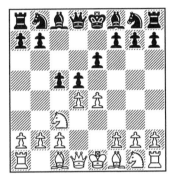

Marshall's tricky variation where it's easy for both sides to get confused.

4.	exd5	exd5
5.	Bb5†	Nc6
6.	Nf3	Nf6
7.	Ne5	Qc7
8.	Bg5	Ne4
9.	Nxd5	....

Tempting 9...Qa5† 10. c3 Qxb5 11. Nc7†.

9.	....	Qd6
10.	Bh4	Qxd5

After this it's mate or loss of the queen. Black should go 10...g7-g5; then White has something to think about.

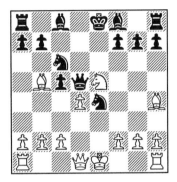

11.	Bc4	Qxd4
12.	Bxf7#	1-0

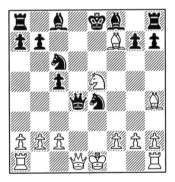

Black has opted to be checkmated rather than lose his queen. It's the parallel bishops mating pattern.

104. FRENCH DEFENSE

1.	e4	e6
2.	d4	d5
3.	Nc3	Nf6
4.	e5	Nfd7
5.	Bd3	Nb6

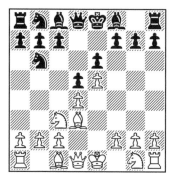

Too passive. He has to strike at the center, ...c7-c5, before White becomes too powerful on the king-side.

6.	Qg4	N8d7
7.	Bg5	Be7
8.	Nf3	0-0

He thinks he's castling into safety, when in fact he's castling into danger. The following move by White is a double threat; mate on h7 or win of the e7-bishop.

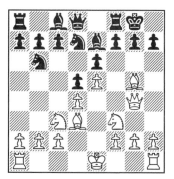

9.	Qh4	f6
10.	Qxh7†	Kf7
11.	Bg6#	1-0

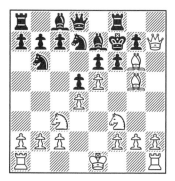

It looks like Black has been check-mated.

105. FRENCH DEFENSE

1.	e4	e6
2.	d4	d5
3.	Nc3	Nf6
4.	Bg5	Be7
5.	e5	Nfd7

White could play 6. Bxe7, but he prefers to gambit a pawn for the attack.

6.	h4	Bxg5
7.	hxg5	Qxg5
8.	Nh3	Qh6

Safer 8...Qe7. From h6 he pins the knight, but soon the knight gets unpinned.

9.	g3	a6
10.	Bg2	f6

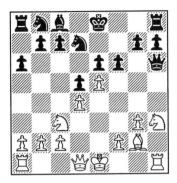

10...g7-g6 gives the queen an escape hatch.

11.	Nf4	Qg5
12.	Rh5	....

The Black queen is trapped and lost.

106. FRENCH DEFENSE

1.	e4	e6
2.	d4	d5
3.	Nc3	Nf6
4.	Bg5	Be7
5.	e5	Nfd7
6.	h4	Bxg5
7.	hxg5	Qxg5
8.	Nh3	Qe7

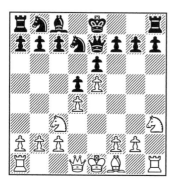

An extra pawn versus the attack. It's supposed to be about even, but in practice White usually wins.

9.	Nf4	Nf8
10.	Qg4	g6

He should play 9...g6 right away. Now it's too late.

11. Nfxd5 ....

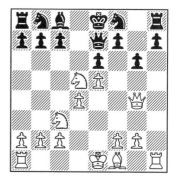

Exploiting the pin of the e6-pawn; 11...exd5 gets slammed by 12. Qxc8†. Relatively best is 11...Qd8 12. Nf6† but then White has his pawn back, plus the attack.

TRAP OF THE DAY:
Double Queen Pawn Openings

107. QUEEN PAWN

1.	d4	d5
2.	Qd3	e6
3.	Qc3	c6

White's last two moves serve no purpose. With his next three moves, he does have a plan. It's just that the plan is not very good.

4.	b3	Nd7
5.	Ba3	Qg5
6.	Bxf8	....

An unguarding error. One moment the bishop guards a key square, the next moment, after it moves, it doesn't. Correct was 6. Nf3 developing and attacking Black's queen.

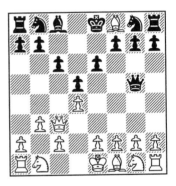

6.	....	Qc1#
	0-1	

Checkmate on the home rank. Curiously, Black never takes anything in this game.

108. QUEEN PAWN

1. d4   d5

The game begins in a normal way, but you won't find White's next three moves in the books.

2. f3   Bf5
3. Be3   e6
4. Bf2   ....

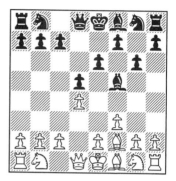

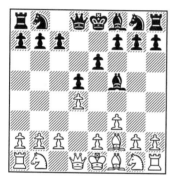

White's bishop deployment has defensive potential, but it's not much use for the attack. This fact seems to have lulled Black to sleep, for he now makes a serious error.

4. ....   g6

Without any prompting, Black locks his bishop in a cage. Why did he do that?

5. g4   ....

The Black bishop is trapped and lost.

109. QUEEN PAWN

1.	d4	d5
2.	c3	c6
3.	Nd2	Nd7

So far everything is perfectly symmetrical. But now White, by virtue of his first move advantage, gets to break open the center.

4.	e4	dxe4
5.	Nxe4	Ndf6
6.	Bd3	Bf5

Attacks the e4-knight, but nothing guards the bishop. Black is wide open for a discovery. He should give preference to the knights: 6...Nxe4 7. Bxe4 Nf6. The c8-bishop can come out later.

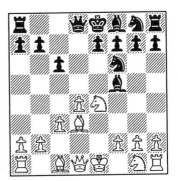

7.	Nxf6†	Nxf6
8.	Bxf5	....

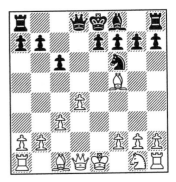

White has won a bishop for nothing.

110. QUEEN PAWN

1.	d4	d5
2.	Bg5	c5
3.	e3	Qc7
4.	Nf3	Bg4
5.	Nbd2	Nc6
6.	c3	e5
7.	dxe5	Nxe5

10.	Nxc6	a6
11.	Nb4†	axb5
12.	Nxd5	....

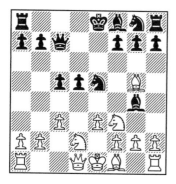

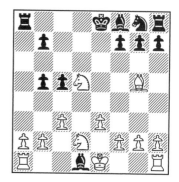

The complications have subsided and White comes out ahead in material. Either the knight forks at c7, or the king takes at d1. Black can't stop both possibilities.

Black relies too heavily on his pin of the f3-knight, not realizing that in the present circumstances the knight can move. That likely explains his premature aggression on move 6. Note also that 7...Bxf3 8. Nxf3 Nxe5 9. Nxe5 Qxe5 fails outright, to 10. Bb5#

8.	Nxe5	Bxd1
9.	Bb5†	Qc6

A forced interposition to save the king. If 10. Bxc6† bxc6 11. Kxd1 f6, so...

111. QUEEN PAWN

1. d4   d5
2. Bg5   Qd6

To unpin the e7-pawn. But after White's next move a new opportunity arises.

3. Nd2   ....

Safer is 3. c2-c3. But the knight move is not necessarily bad.

3. ....   Qb4

The queen attacks two White pawns, at b2 and d4. Trying to cover by 4. Nb3 is illegal as the knight is pinned. So one of the pawns is lost.

This is one of those borderline traps. After 4. Ngf3 Qxb2, White has a lead in development which, to some extent, is compensation for the lost pawn.

112. QUEEN PAWN

1.	d4	d5
2.	Bf4	c6
3.	e3	Nf6
4.	Nc3	Qb6

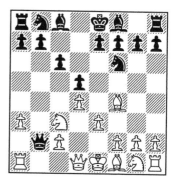

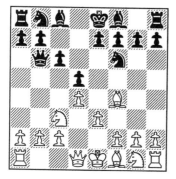

When the bishop leaves c1, b2 lacks a defender. Black tries to take advantage.

5. a3 ....

White seemingly ignores the threat.

5. .... Qxb2

Black pursues his plan with fateful consistency not realizing that the b2-pawn is poisoned. A better move was 5...Bc8-f5.

6. Na4 ....

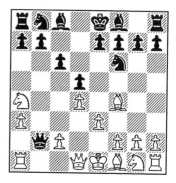

The queen has fallen into a trap and has nowhere to go. The best chance now is to take the rook and just keep fighting.

113. QUEEN PAWN

1.	d4	d5
2.	Nc3	Nc6
3.	Bf4	....

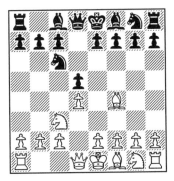

Developing the pieces but with a threat.

3.	....	g6

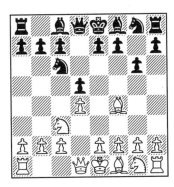

Black is driving blind. He should turn his headlights on. Then he might see what's going on and play 3...a7-a6. That would stop White in his tracks.

4.	Nb5	....

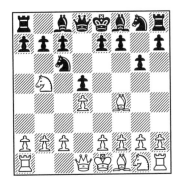

A combined attack on the c7-square. White threatens to win by 5. Nxc7† Kd7 6. Nxa8. The best defense is 4...e7-e5 closing down the bishop's diagonal. That leaves Black minus a pawn after 5. d4xe5, but it's better than losing a rook.

114. QUEEN PAWN

1.	d4	d5
2.	Nc3	e6
3.	e3	Bb4
4.	Nf3	c5
5.	a3	....

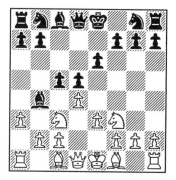

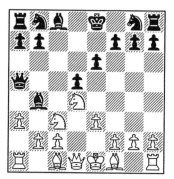

7.	axb4	Qxa1
8.	Nb3	....

The attack on the bishop has far reaching consequences. Here, or on the next move, Black could trade, ...Bxc3† but he prefers counterattack.

5.	....	cxd4
6.	Nxd4	Qa5

This is a mistake. The pin of the a3-pawn is deceptive. The real problem is that Black has not seen far enough ahead.

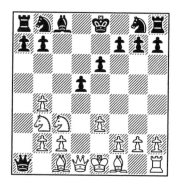

Black's queen is trapped in the corner. There's no way out as all the escape routes are covered.

115. QUEEN PAWN

1. d4	d5
2. e3	Bf5
3. Bd3	e6
4. Bxf5	exf5
5. Qd3	....

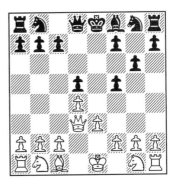

A double-barreled move. The queen attacks in two distinct directions.

5. .... g6

Black sees only in the direction of the f5-pawn. Had he looked along the a6-f1 diagonal, he might have come up with 5...Qd7. Then everything is safely protected.

6. Qb5† ....

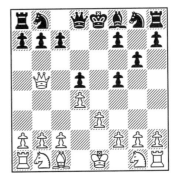

Forking b7/e8. However Black decides to get out of check, he must still lose a pawn. White will take it, because other things being equal, an extra pawn is an advantage.

116. QUEEN PAWN

1.	d4	d5
2.	e3	c5
3.	Bd3	Nc6

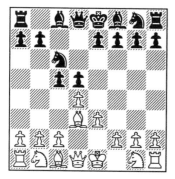

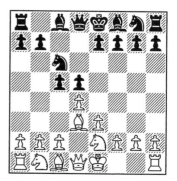

4. .... c4

Aggressive play by Black who is trying to steal the initiative. It's like he's playing a Queen's Gambit, but with colors reversed. The immediate threat is to take twice on d4, winning a pawn.

4. Ne2 ....

Playing the knight to e2 puts a second guard on the d4-pawn, but creates a brand new problem for White. The knight should have gone to f3. Also pretty solid was 4. c2-c3.

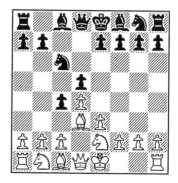

The White bishop is trapped, hemmed in by his own guys. That's what happens when you jam your pieces up.

117. QUEEN PAWN

1.	d4	d5
2.	e3	Bf5
3.	Nc3	Nc6
4.	Bd2	Nf6
5.	Ne2	....

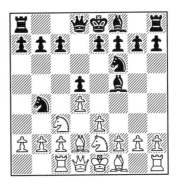

6.	....	Bxc2
7.	Rxc2	Nd3#
	0-1	

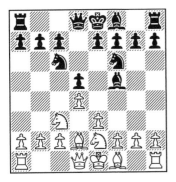

White jams himself up. Playing the knight to e2 blocks in his f1-bishop and leaves his king without any squares. The much better move was 5. Nf3.

5.	....	Nb4
6.	Rc1	....

Figuring on 6...Nxc2† 7. Rxc2 Bxc2 8. Qxc2 when White has two pieces for a rook and pawn. But Black reverses the move order.

It's a smothered checkmate by the Black knight.

118. QUEEN PAWN

1.	d4	d5
2.	f4	....

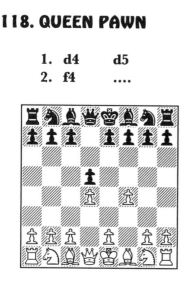

The characteristic move of the Stonewall Attack. The long range plan is to get a grip on the e5-square and then launch a kingside attack. However, it's only dangerous if Black lets it become dangerous.

2.	....	Be6

Weak. The right square for the bishop was f5, looking to take advantage of the hole White created on e4.

3.	Qd3	Nd7

Two weak moves in a row are enough to lose a piece.

4.	f5	....

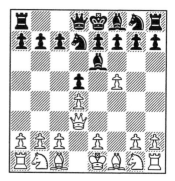

Black blocked in his own bishop. Now the bishop is attacked by a pawn and has nowhere to go. White wins a bishop.

119. QUEEN PAWN

1.	d4	d5
2.	Nf3	b6

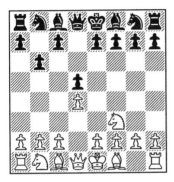

This move is not really called for. The c8-bishop already has a diagonal to come out on, the c8-h3 diagonal. It doesn't need another one. But once he's played ...b7-b6, he has to follow through: ...Bc8-b7. Otherwise c6 is weak and may become an invasion square for the enemy.

3. Ne5   Nd7

Naturally Black wants to challenge the opposing knight. But what about the invasion square? Black didn't take that into account.

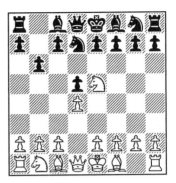

4.	Nc6	....

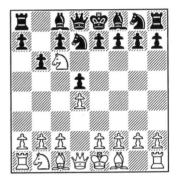

The Black queen is attacked and lost. And she never moved off her starting square.

120. QUEEN PAWN

1.	d4	d5
2.	Nf3	Bf5

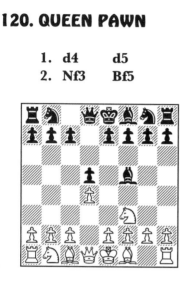

The bishop development might be a tad premature. To prove it White has to play energetically: 3. c4 e6 4. Qb3, pressuring both b7 and d5. But White takes his good old time. And when he finally gets around to attacking b7, Black just ignores it. You'll see why shortly.

3.	e3	Nc6
4.	c3	e6
5.	Qb3	a6
6.	Qxb7	....

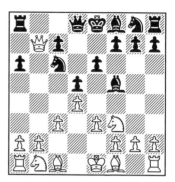

6.	....	Na5

The queen is lost. That's the danger of taking the queen knight pawn with the queen. It's a rare day when White can do it and get away with it. This was not one of those days.

121. QUEEN PAWN

1.	d4	d5
2.	Nf3	e6
3.	Bf4	c6
4.	e3	Nd7
5.	Bd3	....

5.	....	Qf6

There's nothing wrong with Black's play through the first four moves. But f6 should be reserved for bringing out the king-knight, not the queen. Playing the queen to this square is just asking for trouble. And trouble is what Black gets.

6.	Bg5	....

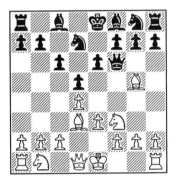

A little one square slide with the bishop and suddenly the Black queen is dead. You bring the queen out early, you lose the queen out early. That's how it goes.

122. QUEEN PAWN

1.	d4	d5
2.	Nf3	e6
3.	Bf4	c5
4.	e3	....

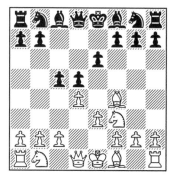

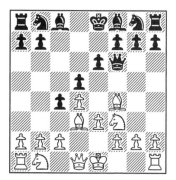

Black's early play is just fine. But look what he does on move four.

4. ....   Qf6

This is anti-chess. You leave the queen at home and put the knight on f6.

5. Bd3   c4

Two mistakes in a row. That's all it takes to lose the game.

6. Bg5   ....

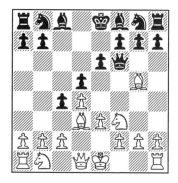

The queen is trapped and lost. It's an old song with lots of different verses. White gets to sing this one.

123. QUEEN PAWN

1.	d4	d5
2.	Nf3	Nf6
3.	Bg5	Nbd7
4.	e3	Ne4
5.	Nbd2	Nxg5
6.	Nxg5	....

7.	Ne6	fxe6
8.	Qh5†	g6
9.	Qxg6#	1-0

Black is doing okay. He can continue 6...e5 or 6...Nf6. Instead his nerves get the better of him.

6. .... h6

Figuring on driving the knight back, Black fatally weakens g6 Naturally, the White knight does not retreat. It goes forward.

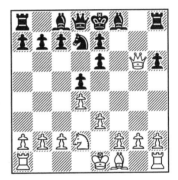

Checkmate takes place along the e8-h5 diagonal. It's another version of the Fool's Mate.

124. QUEEN PAWN

1.	d4	d5
2.	Nf3	Nf6
3.	Bg5	e6
4.	e3	Bb4†
5.	c3	Ba5
6.	Ne5	Bb6
7.	Bd3	0-0
8.	Qf3	Nc6

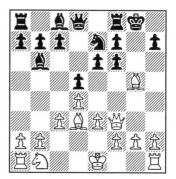

Black has been misplacing his pieces all along. The bishop should have gone to e7, and the b8-knight to d7. Now Black gets overpowered on f6 and his castled position collapses.

9.	Ng4	Ne7
10.	Nxf6†	gxf6

11.	Bxh7†	Kxh7
12.	Qh5†	Kg7
13.	Qh6†	Kg8
14.	Bxf6	Nf5
15.	Qh8#	1-0

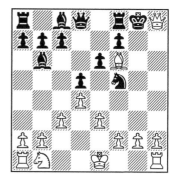

Checkmate is the most likely scenario.

125. QUEEN PAWN

1. d4	d6
2. Nf3	Bg4
3. Nbd2	Bxf3
4. Nxf3	g6
5. e4	c5
6. dxc5	dxc5

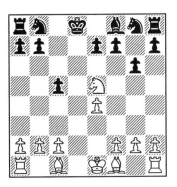

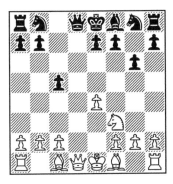

The right way to get the pawn back was 6...Qa5† and 7...Qxc5. After the text move, White trades queens and then takes advantage of Black's king position.

7. Qxd8†	Kxd8
8. Ne5	....

If 8...Nh6? then 9. Bxh6 Bxh6 10. Nxf7† wins.

8.	Ke8
9. Bb5†	Nc6
10. Bxc6†	bxc6
11. Nxc6	....

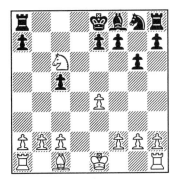

White has won a pawn. He could also have played 10. Nxc6.

126. QUEEN'S GAMBIT

1.	d4	d5
2.	c4	dxc4
3.	e4	b5

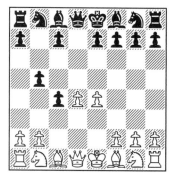

In the coming play, Black tries to support his c4-pawn and White tries to undermine the support.

4.	a4	c6
5.	axb5	cxb5
6.	b3	Ba6

The bishop move runs into a combination. The better play was to let the c4-pawn go: 6...a5 7. bxc4 b4.

7.	bxc4	bxc4

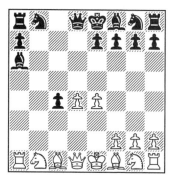

8.	Rxa6	Nxa6
9.	Qa4†	Qd7
10.	Qxa6	....

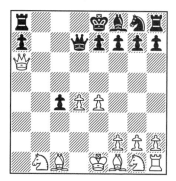

White comes out ahead with two pieces for the rook. Plus the c4-pawn is indefensible, so White will shortly get that as well.

127. QUEEN'S GAMBIT

1. d4	d5
2. c4	dxc4
3. e3	b5
4. a4	....

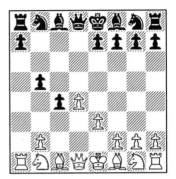

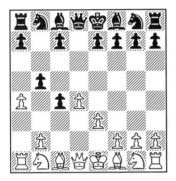

A natural recapture. Here it's a mistake because the long diagonal becomes weak. He has to let the pawn go and cut his loses.

6. Qf3	Nc6
7. Qxc6†	....

Black pursues the wrong plan. There is no way to stop White from getting his pawn back, so Black shouldn't even try.

4.	c6

4...a6 fails to 5. axb5 axb5 6. Rxa8. 4...bxa4 is met by 5. Qxa4† and 6. Qxc4.

5. axb5	cxb5

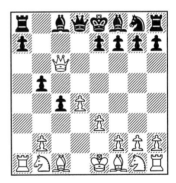

White wins a piece.

128. QUEEN'S GAMBIT

1.	d4	d5
2.	c4	dxc4
3.	e3	Nc6
4.	Bxc4	Na5

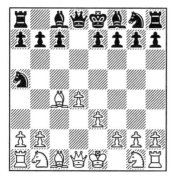

Looking to chase the bishop from its attacking diagonal, Black places his knight on the edge of the board. That's rarely a good idea, and here it is made worse because there's no one guarding the knight. Probably he should just bring out a new piece, 4...Nf6. That's what you're supposed to do in the opening, bring out new pieces, not move the same ones over and over again.

| 5. | Bxf7† | Kxf7 |

| 6. | Qh5† | g6 |
| 7. | Qxa5 | .... |

White picks off the undefended knight and emerges with an extra pawn. In addition Black can no longer castle.

129. QUEEN'S GAMBIT

1.	d4	d5
2.	c4	dxc4
3.	Nf3	Bg4
4.	e3	e6
5.	Bxc4	Nf6
6.	Nc3	Nc6
7.	0-0	Bd6
8.	Be2	0-0
9.	e4	....

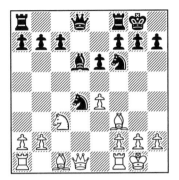

White should let it go at that. His next move compounds the error.

11.	Qxd4	Bxh2†
12.	Kxh2	Qxd4

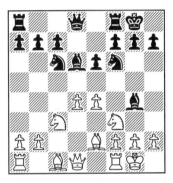

The advance of the e-pawn is badly timed because it leaves the d4-pawn insufficiently defended.

9.	....	Bxf3
10.	Bxf3	Nxd4

Black has won a pawn.

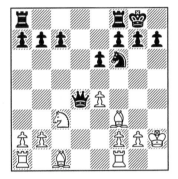

Black has won the queen.

130. QUEEN'S GAMBIT

1.	d4	d5
2.	c4	dxc4
3.	Nf3	Nc6
4.	g3	....

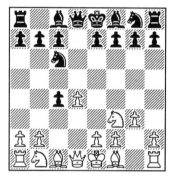

Normal is 4. e4 and the bishop comes out on the a6-f1 diagonal, taking the pawn at c4. It's hard to say if flanking the bishop is really better, but in this game at least, it works.

4.	....	Bg4
5.	Bg2	Bxf3
6.	Bxf3	Qxd4

If he wants to take the d4-pawn, then he should do it with his knight, 6...Nxd4. Capturing with the queen is bad because White can knock out the support.

7.	Bxc6†	bxc6
8.	Qxd4	....

White has won the queen.

131. QUEEN'S GAMBIT

1.	d4	d5
2.	c4	dxc4
3.	Nf3	c5
4.	e3	cxd4
5.	Bxc4	....

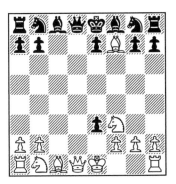

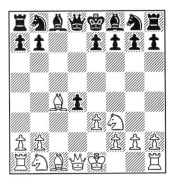

5. .... dxe3

A greedy pawn grab which opens the d-file and allows a combination. He should just develop, 5...Nf6.

6. Bxf7† ....

A deflection sacrifice to draw the king away from the queen. The Black king can't be in two places at the same time.

6.	....	Kxf7
7.	Qxd8	....

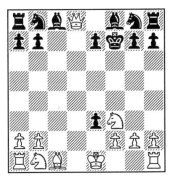

White gains the queen for a bishop. That's always a good trade if you're on the winning side.

132. QUEEN'S GAMBIT

1.	d4	d5
2.	c4	dxc4
3.	Nf3	Nf6
4.	e3	g6
5.	Bxc4	Bg4

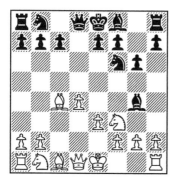

Not a good idea. White has too many ways to take advantage of the bishop move. Correct was 5...Bg7 followed by castling.

6. Ne5 ....

Another way was 6. Bxf7+ Kxf7 7. Ne5+ Ke8 8. Nxg4. And there's also 6. Qb3 with a double threat to b7 and f7.

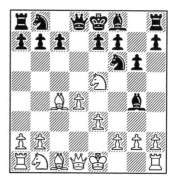

6. .... Bxd1

Taking the queen loses on the spot. The best chance was 6...Be6.

7. Bxf7# 1-0

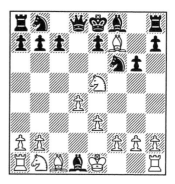

Black is checkmated.

133. QUEEN'S GAMBIT

1.	d4	d5
2.	c4	dxc4
3.	Nf3	Nf6
4.	e3	e6
5.	Bxc4	c5
6.	Qe2	cxd4
7.	exd4	Nbd7

9.	Nxf7	Kxf7
10.	Qxe6†	Kg6
11.	Bd3†	Kh5
12.	Qh3#	1-0

Better to hold off on this move. Priority should be given to getting castled: 7...Be7 and then 8...0-0.

8. Ne5   Be7

Now this is too slow. The way to castle was by 8...Bb4† and then ...0-0.

Black's king has been hunted down and checkmated.

134. QUEEN'S GAMBIT

1.	d4	d5
2.	c4	e5

Albin's Counter Gambit which leads to trappy play.

3.	dxe5	d4

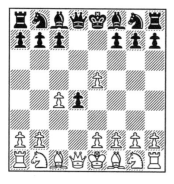

4.	e3	....

This natural looking move is known to be weak. He should play 4. Nf3.

4.	....	Bb4†
5.	Bd2	dxe3
6.	Bxb4	....

Missing Black's seventh move.

He had to play 6. fxe3.

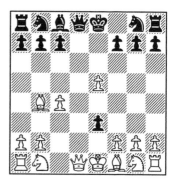

6.	....	exf2†
7.	Ke2	fxg1/N†
8.	Rxg1	Bg4†

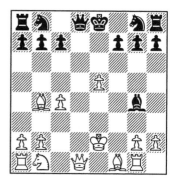

A skewer on the king and queen. After White moves his king, Black takes the queen.

135. QUEEN'S GAMBIT

1.	d4	d5
2.	c4	Nc6

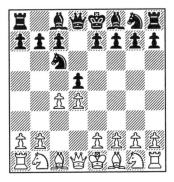

An invention of the Russian Grand Master Mikhail Tchigorin, who seems to be the only one who understood how to play it. Everyone else who tried this defense ran into trouble.

3. Nc3   Be6

Already Black goes wrong. He should either take, 3...dxc4 or else defend by 3...e6. Now White knocks the props out from under Black's center.

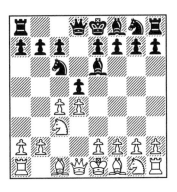

4.	cxd5	Bxd5
5.	e4	Be6
6.	d5	....

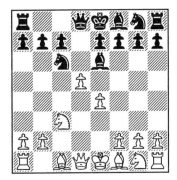

And the pawn fork assures the win of a piece. It's Black's choice which piece he wants to lose, bishop or knight. Great choice.

136. QUEEN'S GAMBIT

1.	d4	d5
2.	c4	Nf6
3.	cxd5	Nxd5
4.	e4	Nb4

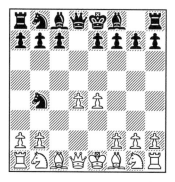

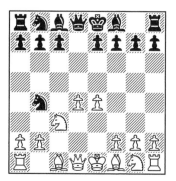

5.	....	Qxd4
6.	Qxd4	Nc2†
7.	Kd1	Nxd4

Safest is for the knight to drop back to f6 or b6. What he plays shouldn't work. But when White gets complacent, Black gets away with it.

5. Nc3 ....

The correct move was 5. Qa4† N4c6 6. d5 winning a piece. Now it's Black's turn to show what he can do.

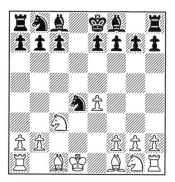

Black has recovered his queen and emerges a pawn ahead.

137. QUEEN'S GAMBIT

1.	d4	d5
2.	c4	Nf6
3.	cxd5	Qxd5
4.	Nc3	Qd8
5.	e4	e6
6.	e5	Nd5
7.	Nf3	Nd7
8.	Bd3	c6
9.	Ng5	h6
10.	Qh5	Qe7
11.	Nxf7	....

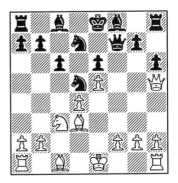

12. Bg6 ....

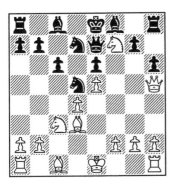

White is pressing hard. Does Black have a reply?

11. .... Qxf7

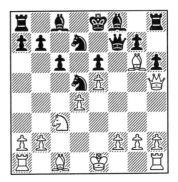

Pins and wins the queen.

Taking loses instantly. He might have tried 11...N5f6 12. exf6 Nxf6. Then after 13. Q-moves Qxf7. But White in turn has 12. Nd6† a double check.

138. QUEEN'S GAMBIT

1.	d4	d5
2.	c4	e6
3.	Bf4	c6
4.	e3	Be7
5.	a3	a5
6.	Nf3	Qd7

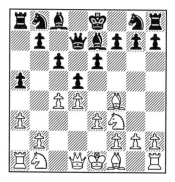

This, along with Black's next two moves, don't make much sense. Black is playing without a plan, just moving pieces around.

7.	Nbd2	Bd8
8.	Nb3	Ne7

The third weak move of the sequence is the worst. The knight should have gone to f6. Playing to e7, he jams himself up.

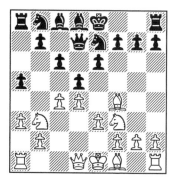

| 9. | Nc5 | .... |

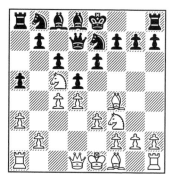

The queen is trapped and lost. This is what happens when you shuttle pieces around to no purpose.

139. QUEEN'S GAMBIT

1.	d4	d5
2.	c4	e6
3.	Nf3	c5
4.	dxc5	....

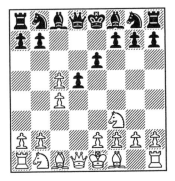

Better to take at d5. The text helps Black develop his bishop.

4.	....	Bxc5
5.	cxd5	Nf6

He could take back right away, 5...exd5. By delaying the recapture, Black sets a little trap. And White falls right in to it.

| 6. | dxe6 | .... |

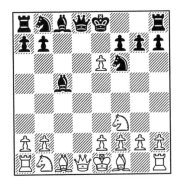

Opens the d-file with fatal effect. Correct was 6. e3.

6.	....	Bxf2†
7.	Kxf2	Qxd1

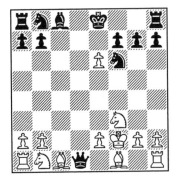

Black wins queen for bishop. Good for Black; bad for White.

140. QUEEN'S GAMBIT

1.	d4	d5
2.	c4	e6
3.	Nf3	c5
4.	dxc5	Bxc5
5.	Nbd2	....

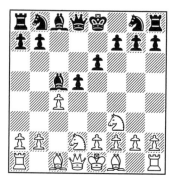

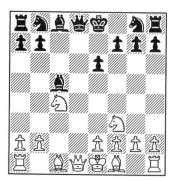

| 6. | .... | Bxf2† |
| 7. | Kxf2 | Qxd1 |

To protect the c4-pawn in case Black takes ...dxc4. A simpler way was 5. e3 and the f1-bishop can retake.

| 5. | .... | dxc4 |
| 6. | Nxc4 | .... |

White follows his plan, not realizing that something is wrong. The right way to get the pawn back was by 6. Qa4† and 7. Qxc4.

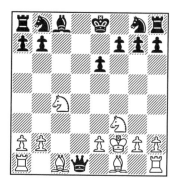

The bishop deflection sacrifice has netted Black the queen. A fine investment.

141. QUEEN'S GAMBIT

1.	d4	d5
2.	c4	e6
3.	Nf3	Nf6
4.	Bg5	Be7
5.	e3	0-0
6.	Nbd2	b6
7.	Bd3	Nc6

Better 7...Bc8-b7. In the Queen's Gambit it's not a good idea to block the c7-pawn with the knight. Black gets away with it for a while, but later pays the price for not knowing the concept.

8.	cxd5	Nb4
9.	Bb1	exd5

10.	a3	Nc6

Here, he had to drop back to a6.

11.	Bxf6	Bxf6
12.	Qc2	....

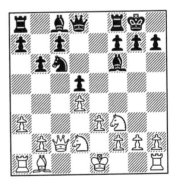

Mate at h7 or else he wins the c6-knight.

142. QUEEN'S GAMBIT

1.	d4	d5
2.	c4	e6
3.	Nc3	Nf6
4.	Bf4	c5
5.	Nb5	....

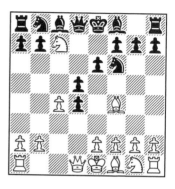

Threatens 6. Nc7+ forking king and rook. Black could defend by 5...Na6, but he doesn't have to just yet. He can set a trap.

5.	....	cxd4
6.	Nxc7†	....

White doesn't see it. If he had, he would take back on d4.

6.	....	Qxc7
7.	Bxc7	Bb4†
8.	Qd2	Bxd2†
9.	Kxd2	dxc4

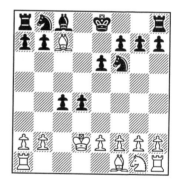

Black has recovered his queen and emerges two pawns ahead.

143. QUEEN'S GAMBIT

1.	d4	d5
2.	c4	e6
3.	Nc3	Nf6
4.	Nf3	Bb4

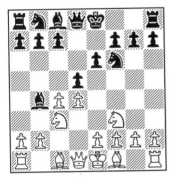

Leads to thrust and parry play. Both sides have to stay alert.

5.	Qa4†	Nc6
6.	cxd5	Qxd5
7.	g3	Qc4
8.	e4	....

White thinks he's winning the queen. In fact, it's just the reverse. White should play 8. Bd2; then he's safe.

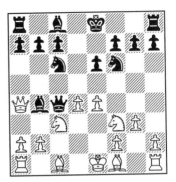

8.	....	Bxc3†
9.	bxc3	Qxa4

After knocking out the c3-knight with check, there's nothing guarding White's queen. Black removes it from the board.

144. QUEEN'S GAMBIT

1.	d4	d5
2.	c4	e6
3.	Nc3	Nf6
4.	cxd5	Nxd5
5.	Nxd5	exd5
6.	Bf4	g5

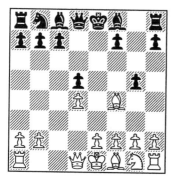

A provocative pawn thrust to see if White will misplace his bishop.

7. Be5 ....

White misplaces his bishop. The attack on the h8-rook was too tempting and White became blind to the real danger. The right move was 7. Bd2.

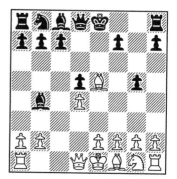

7. .... Bb4†

Whoops! Now the only way to save the king is to block with the queen.

8. Qd2 Bxd2†

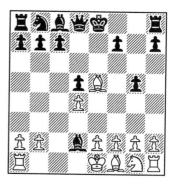

Black wins the queen.

145. QUEEN'S GAMBIT

1.	d4	d5
2.	c4	e6
3.	Nc3	Nf6
4.	cxd5	exd5
5.	Bf4	Be7
6.	e3	c6
7.	Qc2	Nbd7
8.	0-0-0	Nh5

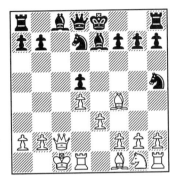

10. Bc7 ....

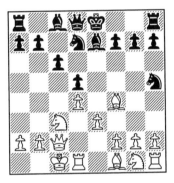

The f4-bishop is strong and Black goes after it. But his timing is all wrong.

9. Nxd5 cxd5

Two mistakes in a row is one too many. He should settle for the loss of a pawn after 9...Nxf4 10. Nxf4. That way he gets rid of the bishop before it can do more harm.

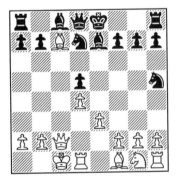

The harmful bishop traps the queen.

155

146. QUEEN'S GAMBIT

1.	d4	d5
2.	c4	e6
3.	Nc3	Nf6
4.	Bg5	Nbd7
5.	cxd5	cxd5
6.	Nxd5	....

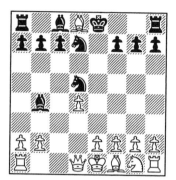

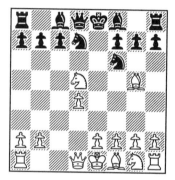

Figuring that the f6-knight is pinned and can't take. But what if he can take? Then White should have played 6. e2-e3 instead.

6.	....	Nxd5
7.	Bxd8	Bb4†

White has captured the queen; now it's Black turn. Attacking the king, he gets the queen back with interest.

8.	Qd2	Bxd2†
9.	Kxd2	Kxd8

Count everything up and you find that Black is a piece ahead.

147. QUEEN'S GAMBIT

1. d4	d5
2. c4	e6
3. Nc3	Nf6
4. Bg5	Be7
5. e3	Ne4
6. Bxe7	Qxe7
7. Bd3	Nxc3
8. bxc3	c5
9. Ne2	cxd4
10. cxd4	dxc4
11. Bxc4	Qb4†
12. Qd2	....

13. ....   Qxc1

Worse was 13...Qd5? 14. Rxc8+ Ke7 15. Rxh8.

14. Qxc1   ....

White has won the queen for a rook and a minor piece.

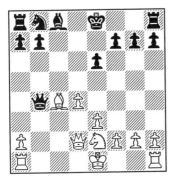

12. ....   Qxc4

Black sets himself up for a skewer. Best was ...Qxd2†

13. Rc1   ....

148. QUEEN'S GAMBIT

1.	d4	d5
2.	c4	c6
3.	cxd5	cxd5
4.	Nf3	Nf6
5.	Nc3	Nc6
6.	Qd3	g6
7.	e4	dxe4
8.	Nxe4	Nxe4
9.	Qxe4	Qa5†
10.	Bd2	Bf5

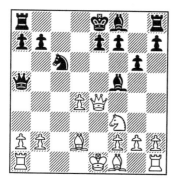

Black's last move proposes an even trade. "You take my queen, I take your queen." White is agreeable, but he adds a little refinement, an in-between-check, which Black overlooked.

11.	Qxc6†	....

11.	....	bxc6
12.	Bxa5	....

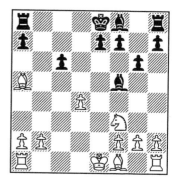

The queens are off the board and so too is Black's queen-knight. White has won a piece.

149. QUEEN'S GAMBIT

1.	d4	d5
2.	c4	c6
3.	e3	Bf5
4.	c5	Bxb1

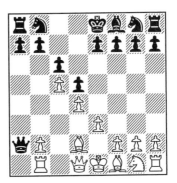

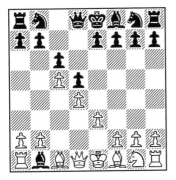

The start of a plan to win a pawn. There's only one problem; Black outsmarts himself.

5.	Rxb1	Qa5†
6.	Bd2	Qxa2

Black could still back out and not take the pawn. Once he takes on a2, it's too late.

7. Bc3 ....

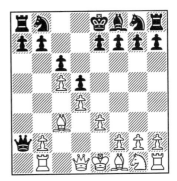

Guards the b2-pawn and sets up for 8. Ra1, trapping Black's queen. Black can do whatever he wants on move 7, but his queen is not going to escape.

150. QUEEN'S GAMBIT

1.	d4	d5
2.	c4	c6
3.	Nf3	Bf5
4.	Qb3	Qb6
5.	cxd5	Qxb3
6.	axb3	Bxb1

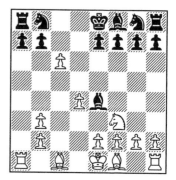

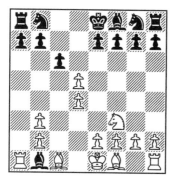

On 6...cxd5, Black did not like 7. Nc3, threatening both 8. Nxd5 and 8. Nb5. So he gets rid of the knight.

7. dxc6   Be4

Black seems to have everything under control. Plus he has an extra piece.

8.	Rxa7	Rxa7
9.	c7	....

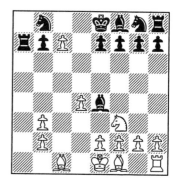

White makes a new queen next move. It happens at b8 or c8. Black can't cover both squares.

151. QUEEN'S GAMBIT

1.	d4	d5
2.	c4	c6
3.	Nf3	Bg4
4.	e3	dxc4
5.	Bxc4	....

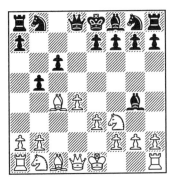

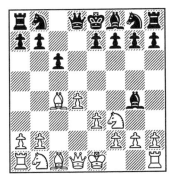

White threatens 6. Qb3 with a double attack on b7 and f7. Black could defend by 5...e7-e6 or perhaps 5...Bxf3 6. Qxf3 e6.

5.	....	b5

But this is no defense at all. White is in position to take advantage of the undefended g4-bishop. All he has to do is arrange matters so he can move his pinned f3-knight.

6.	Bxf7†	Kxf7
7.	Ne5†	Ke8
8.	Qxg4	....

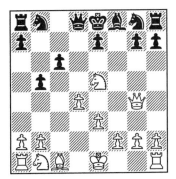

White has won a pawn and Black is no longer able to castle.

152. QUEEN'S GAMBIT

1.	d4	d5
2.	c4	c6
3.	Nc3	dxc4
4.	e4	e5
5.	Bxc4	exd4
6.	Nf3	....

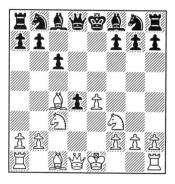

Inviting Black to take the c3-knight. After 6...dxc3 7. Bxf7+ Ke7 8. Qb3 White gets a dangerous attack.

6. .... b5

All the same he should have taken the knight and then tried to ride out the storm. Opening theory says it can be done.

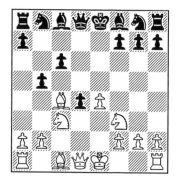

Advancing the b-pawn makes things worse.

7.	Nxb5	cxb5
8.	Bd5	....

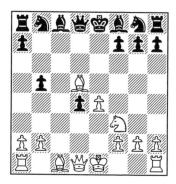

White picks up the rook in the corner, leaving him the exchange ahead.

153. QUEEN'S GAMBIT

1. d4	d5
2. c4	c6
3. Nc3	e6
4. e4	dxe4
5. Nxe4	Bb4†
6. Bd2	Qxd4

After 7. Bxb4 Qxe4+ 8. Be2 White has good attacking chances for his sacrificed pawn. His next move is not quite so good, but Black still has to be careful.

7. Nc3	a5
8. Qh5	Ra6
9. 0-0-0	Qxf2
10. Qg5	g6

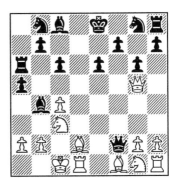

Missing the main threat. He should have played 10...Qf6.

11. Qd8†	Kxd8
12. Bg5†	Kc7
13. Bd8#	1-0

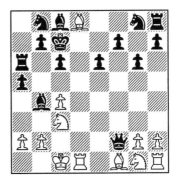

Black is checkmated.

154. QUEEN'S GAMBIT

1. d4	d5
2. c4	c6
3. Nc3	e6
4. Nf3	f6

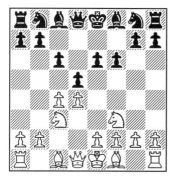

Too many pawn moves. He should play 4...Nf6.

5. Qc2	Ne7
6. e4	Nd7
7. Bd3	b6
8. 0-0	Bb7
9. Re1	a6
10. exd5	exd5

There's no point criticizing Black's individual moves because his whole treatment of the opening is one big mistake. White now closes in for the kill.

11. Bg6†	hxg6
12. Qxg6# 1-0	

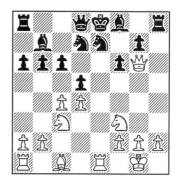

No surprise; Black has been checkmated. That's the penalty for leaving the king uncastled.

155. QUEEN'S GAMBIT

1.	d4	d5
2.	c4	c6
3.	Nf3	e6
4.	Qc2	Bd6
5.	Bg5	Ne7

Black is misplacing his pieces. On move 4 the knight should have come to f6 and on move 5 the bishop to e7. The way he's done it means he has to be careful from here on in.

6. g3   Qc7

Now he's really done it. His bishop is completely jammed in with no place to go.

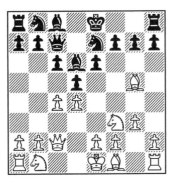

7. c5   Qa5†

Vacates c7 but White gives no time to save the bishop.

8. Bd2   ....

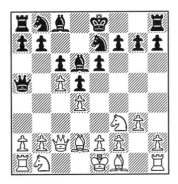

Queen and bishop are under fire. One of them is lost.

156. QUEEN PAWN

1.	d4	d6
2.	Nf3	Bg4
3.	h3	Bxf3
4.	gxf3	Nf6
5.	Nd2	e6
6.	b3	Nd5

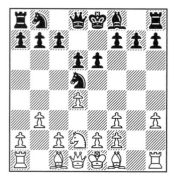

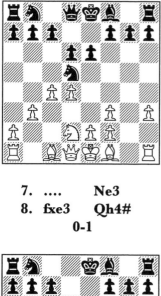

White sees the threat to win the queen (...Nc3) but there is even more danger than he suspects.

7.	c4	....

7.	....	Ne3
8.	fxe3	Qh4#
	0-1	

Leads to loss of the queen or mate. Better was 7. Bb2, or perhaps 7. Ne4, which at least gives the queen some breathing room.

The White king has been checkmated along the Fool's Mate diagonal, e1-h4.

157. QUEEN PAWN

1.	d4	Nc6
2.	d5	Ne5
3.	f4	Ng6

The play is to provoke the advance of White's pawns, hoping they will become overextended. Sometimes the strategy works and sometimes it backfires.

4. Nf3   Nf6

Black makes a routine developing move, overlooking the enemy threat. He has to advance one of his center pawns. Either, 4...d6 or 4...e6. The rule of thumb is that you can't play the opening without moving a center pawn.

5. f5   ....

The g6-knight is trapped and lost. White wins a piece. Moral: move a center pawn before it's too late.

158. QUEEN PAWN

1.	d4	e6
2.	Bf4	Ne7

It's not a good idea to block in the f8-bishop. Probably Black can get away with it so long as he remembers to move the knight again.

3.	Nc3	b6
4.	Nb5	Na6

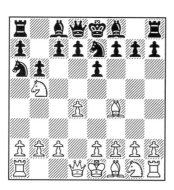

Black sees the threat to the c7-pawn and guards it with his queen-knight. But there's more here than meets the eye. This was a good moment to move the other knight, 4... Ne7-d5. Then Black is safe. Also he could move 4...d7-d6.

5. Bxc7   Nxc7

Else he loses the queen.

6. Nd6#   1-0

It's smothered mate by the knight.

159. QUEEN PAWN

| 1. | d4 | e6 |
| 2. | d5 | .... |

White is trying to establish a pawn wedge in Black's half of the board. The problem is that the pawn is overextended. It's easier for Black to attack it, than it is for White to defend it.

2.	....	Nf6
3.	Bg5	Bc5
4.	Nc3	....

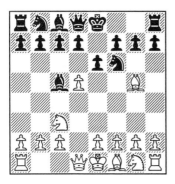

White's moves look quite reasonable, but nothing really works. It all stems from his premature second move.

| 4. | .... | Bxf2† |

| 5. | Kxf2 | Ng4† |
| 6. | Ke1 | Qxg5 |

Black has won a pawn. Also, White has lost his castling rights.

160. QUEEN PAWN

1.	d4	Nf6
2.	Nf3	c5
3.	Bf4	....

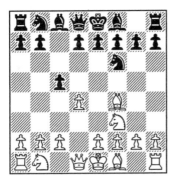

This is an instance where White does better to push, 3. d5, gaining space in the center. It's easy enough to defend the pawn; White has moves like c4 and Nc3.

3.	....	cxd4
4.	Nxd4	....

Like it or not he had to take back with the queen, 4. Qxd4. Taking with the knight, White loses control of the e5-square. Black drives the point home with back to back forks, first a pawn fork and then a queen fork.

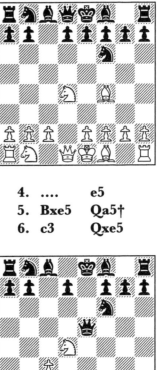

4.	....	e5
5.	Bxe5	Qa5†
6.	c3	Qxe5

Black has won a bishop.

161. QUEEN PAWN

1.	d4	Nf6
2.	Nf3	c5
3.	dxc5	Qa5†
4.	Qd2	Qxc5

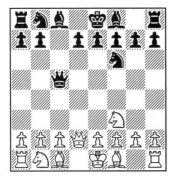

Nothing wrong with Black's play up to here. But after White's next move, things take a turn for the worse.

5. Qc3 ....

Psychological chess. Black is one of those players who can't play without his queen. Probably he can, but he's convinced himself that he can't.

5. .... Qh5

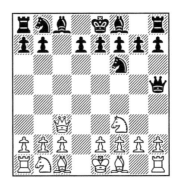

As expected Black shuns the trade of queens.

6. Qxc8# 1-0

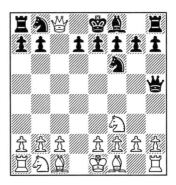

Checkmate. You really have to play the board, not your likes and dislikes.

162. QUEEN PAWN

1.	d4	Nf6
2.	Nf3	c5
3.	c3	b6
4.	Nbd2	d6

For what Black has in mind, this pawn move is unnecessary. In fact, as the game goes, it even proves harmful.

5.	e3	Ba6

Black wants to eliminate the opposing light-squared bishop. A commendable strategy, but the tactical situation is such that it can't be done. Poor Black doesn't see why. Otherwise he'd settle the bishop on b7, where it's safe.

6.	Bxa6	Nxa6
7.	Qa4†	....

Next move the queen picks up the a6-knight, leaving White a piece ahead.

163. QUEEN PAWN

1. d4	Nf6
2. c4	d6
3. Nf3	Bg4
4. Nbd2	Nc6
5. d5	Nb8
6. Qb3	Nfd7
7. Qxb7	....

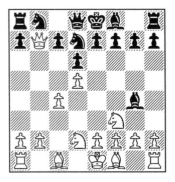

Black had several ways to guard his b7-pawn. But he chose not to defend it. White should have asked himself why? He didn't.

7.	....	Nb6

Guards the a8-rook and seals in the White queen.

8. c5	....

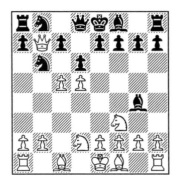

A distraction. If 8...dxc5, 9. d6 and the queen escapes.

8.	....	Bc8

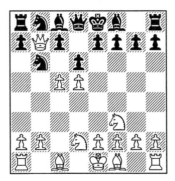

Black, however, will not be distracted. The queen is trapped and lost.

164. BUDAPEST

1.	d4	Nf6
2.	Nd2	e5

Emboldened by White's passive second move, Black offers a gambit.

3.	dxe5	Ng4
4.	h3	....

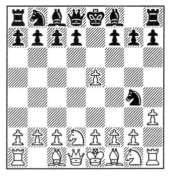

There were no serious threats and White should just develop, 4. Ng1-f3. Instead, he sees ghosts and he panics. Moving the h2-pawn creates a fatal weakness at g3. Black spots the weakness and moves in for the kill.

4.	....	Ne3

Threatens the queen.

5.	fxe3	Qh4†
6.	g3	Qxg3#

0-1

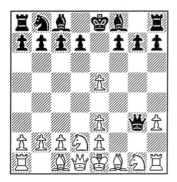

White is checkmated. It's another version of the Fool's Mate.

165. BUDAPEST

1.	d4	Nf6
2.	c4	e5

The tricky Budapest Gambit. White should take the pawn, 3. dxe5. His next two moves are inferior.

3.	d5	Bc5
4.	Bg5	....

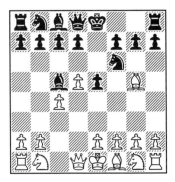

An outright mistake. Black can already gain a pawn by 4...Bxf2† 5. Kxf2 Ne4† forking king and bishop. With his next move, he tries for even more.

4. ....   Ne4

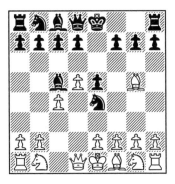

5. Bxd8   ....

Best was 5. Be3 Bxe3 6. fxe3 with a bad game.

5. ....   Bxf2#
0-1

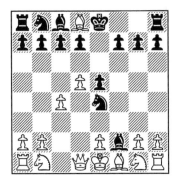

White's king has been checkmated.

166. BUDAPEST

1.	d4	Nf6
2.	c4	e5
3.	dxe5	Ng4
4.	Bf4	Nc6
5.	Nf3	Bb4†
6.	Nbd2	Qe7
7.	a3	Ngxe5

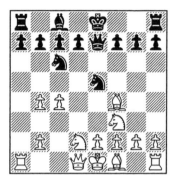

Black has his pawn back, but what about his attacked b4-bishop?

8. axb4 ....

White thinks he's winning a bishop for free. But he's sadly mistaken. He should play 8. Nxe5 Nxe5 9. e3. Then he threatens to take the bishop.

8.	....	Nd3#
	0-1	

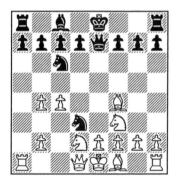

The White king has been checkmated. It's a smothered mate by the knight. Also it's a pin mate as the e2-pawn cannot take the knight.

167. BENONI DEFENSE

1.	d4	c5
2.	dxc5	Qa5†
3.	Nc3	Qxc5
4.	e4	e5

Turns over the d5-square to White's knight. One step with the e-pawn was safer.

5.	Nf3	d6
6.	Nd5	Nf6

Challenging the knight but overlooking the threat to the queen. Something else should have been played. Maybe 6...a7-a6, securing b5. Still, Black's game already looks bad.

7.	b4	Qc6
8.	Bb5	Qxb5
9.	Nc7†	Kd8
10.	Nxb5	....

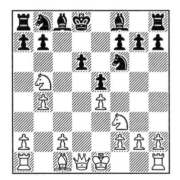

White has won the queen for a bishop.

168. BENONI DEFENSE

1.	d4	c5
2.	d5	e5
3.	Nc3	d6
4.	g3	g6
5.	Bh3	Bg7
6.	Ne4	....

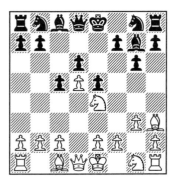

An anti-positional move whose only purpose is to set a trap.

6. .... Nf6

Mechanical development. Black misses the point and falls into the trap. He should take 6...Bxh3, and White has nothing.

7. Bxc8 Nxe4

Or 7...Qxc8 8. Nxd6† forking king and queen.

8. Bxb7 ....

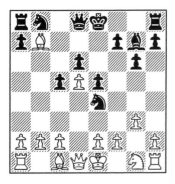

Followed by 9. Bxa8 winning the exchange.

169. BENONI DEFENSE

1.	d4	c5
2.	d5	d6
3.	e4	Nf6
4.	Nc3	g6
5.	Be3	Ng4

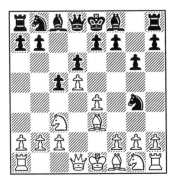

Intending to harass the bishop or take it off. But the knight is vulnerable on g4. Instead, 5...Bg7 and 6...0-0 was the right play.

6.	Bb5†	Bd7
7.	Qxg4	....

White wins a piece as the d7-bishop is pinned and can't take back. From this position one game went...

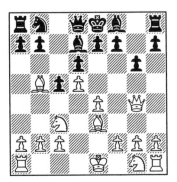

7.	....	Bxb5
8.	Nxb5	Qa5†
9.	Bd2	Qxb5
10.	Qc8#	1-0

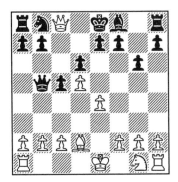

And Black has been checkmated.

170. DUTCH DEFENSE

1.	d4	f5
2.	e4	fxe4

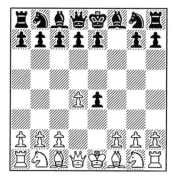

The Staunton Gambit, named after the English Champion of the 1840s.

3.	f3	exf3
4.	Bd3	fxg2

Too greedy. Black has his eye on the h1-rook and subsequent promotion to a queen. But he's run out of time as White strikes first. The correct move was 4...Ng8-f6, which would prevent White's next play.

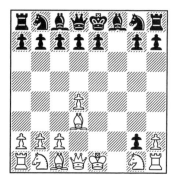

5.	Qh5†	g6
6.	Bxg6†	hxg6
7.	Qxg6#	1-0

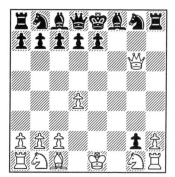

Checkmate along diagonal, e8-h5. This can happen when you play with only your pawns. The pieces must come out.

171. DUTCH DEFENSE

1. d4	f5
2. e4	fxe4
3. Nc3	Nf6
4. Bg5	c5
5. Bxf6	exf6
6. Bc4	exd4
7. Nd5	Qa5†

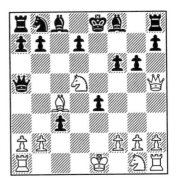

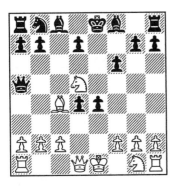

White is playing fast and loose. He wants the attack and he doesn't bother to count pawns.

8. c3	dxc3
9. Qh5†	g6

Blocking the check is inadequate. Here he has to move the king, 9... Kd8.

Then the position is a mess and anything can happen.

10. Nxf6†	Ke7
11. Qxa5	....

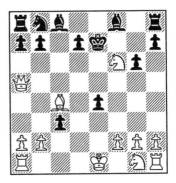

White swoops kingside to queenside and vacuums off Black's queen.

172. DUTCH DEFENSE

1.	d4	f5
2.	Nd2	....

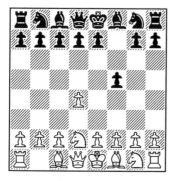

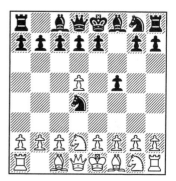

4.	e3	....

White plays a quiet developing move. It's neither good nor bad, merely playable. But it temps Black into playing too aggressively.

2.	....	Nc6
3.	d5	Nd4

A carefree plunge into White's territory. Black has let his guard down. The knight should have stayed on his own side of the board, 3...Ne5 4. f4 Nf7.

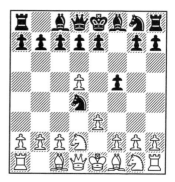

Trapping the knight in midboard. A knight in the center should have eight squares to go to. One square, f5, is occupied, the other seven are all covered by White.

173. DUTCH DEFENSE

1.	d4	f5
2.	Bg5	h6
3.	Bh4	g5
4.	Bg3	f4

It looks like White has gotten his bishop trapped. But it's not that simple. Black's pawns have been lured forward and his king is vulnerable on the e8-h5 diagonal.

5. e3 h5

No time to take the bishop; he has to prevent Qh5#

6. Bd3 Rh6

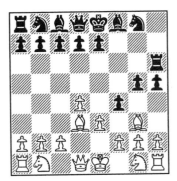

Stops 7. Bg6# but the rook move is insufficient. Better 6...Bg7 making an escape square for the king at f8.

7.	Qxh5†	Rxh5
8.	Bg6#	1-0

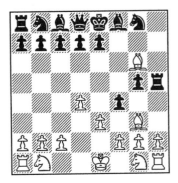

Black is checkmated.

174. DUTCH DEFENSE

1.	d4	f5
2.	e3	e6
3.	Bd3	Nf6
4.	c4	Bd6
5.	Nc3	Ng4

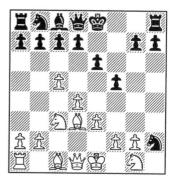

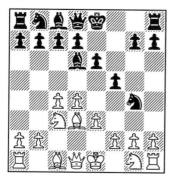

This is too crude to be effective. 6. Nf3 defends but White decides to lure the opponent on.

6.	c5	Bxh2

Black continues as planned not realizing that it favors White.

7.	Rxh2	Nxh2

8.	Qh5†	g6
9.	Qxh2	....

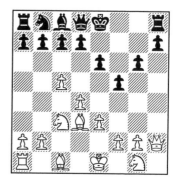

Two minor pieces are superior to rook and pawn in the late opening and middle game. In the endgame things may even out. But we're not there yet.

175. DUTCH DEFENSE

1. d4	f5
2. c4	Nc6

He should give preference to the other knight, 2...Nf6.

3. Nc3	e5
4. d5	Nd4

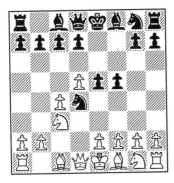

Knights belong in the center, but sometimes you just can't put your knight in the center. Either the opponent won't let you or it's just too risky. Here the best thing for the knight to do is drop back 4...Nce7.

5. e3	....

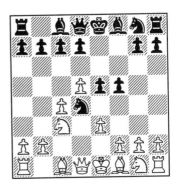

White let the knight come to d4 because he knew there was no way back once it was attack by the e-pawn. Black should have smelled a rat, but he didn't. The upshot is that White wins a knight.

176. DUTCH DEFENSE

1.	d4	f5
2.	c4	Nf6
3.	Nc3	g6
4.	e3	Bg7
5.	Bd2	0-0

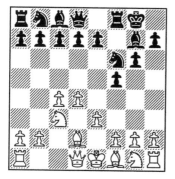

With the bishop flanked on g7, this is the Leningrad Variation of the Dutch, where the d-pawn is supposed to go to d6. But watch what happens.

6. Rc1   d5

There's another line, the Dutch Stonewall, where Black places his pawns on c6 and d5. By mixing up two different systems, Black lands in hot water.

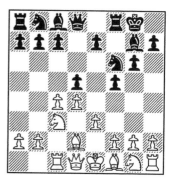

7.	cxd5	Nxd5
8.	Nxd5	Qxd5
9.	Bc4	....

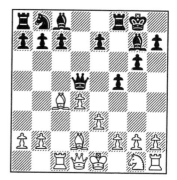

White pins and wins the queen.

177. NIMZO-INDIAN

1.	d4	Nf6
2.	c4	e6
3.	Nc3	Bb4
4.	g3	d5
5.	Bg2	dxc4

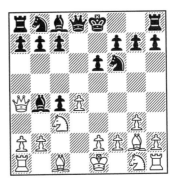

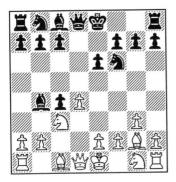

A faulty idea which opens the diagonal for the g2-bishop. Black may have thought he's winning a pawn. But he's not. Castling was certainly better. It gets the king to a place where it is not so easy to attack.

6. Qa4† ....

Forking king and bishop. Black may have relied on his next move, overlooking that his defender can be knocked with a check.

6.	....	Nc6
7.	Bxc6†	bxc6
8.	Qxb4	....

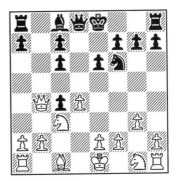

White wins a minor piece.

187

178. NIMZO-INDIAN

1.	d4	Nf6
2.	c4	e6
3.	Nc3	Bb4
4.	Bd2	b6
5.	a3	Bd6
6.	e3	Ba6
7.	f3	Nd5

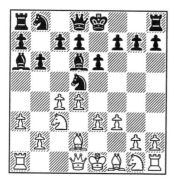

This last move has no strategic motive I can think of. It's main point is to bait a trap. Maybe White will take the knight?

8. cxd5 ....

White sees a knight; White takes a knight. That's not good enough. What he has to do is make provision for the coming queen check.

8.	....	Qh4†
9.	g3	Bxg3†
10.	hxg3	Qxg3#

0-1

White is checkmated.

179. NIMZO-INDIAN

1. d4	Nf6
2. c4	e6
3. Nc3	Bb4
4. e3	b6
5. Nf3	Bb7
6. Bd3	Ne4
7. Qc2	f5
8. 0-0	Bxc3
9. bxc3	0-0
10. Nd2	Qh4

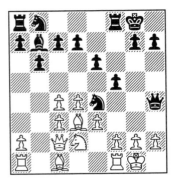

A typical Nimzo-Indian fight is taking shape for control of e4. Ultimately White should prevail, as he can always arrange to play his pawn up to f3.

11. g3	Ng5

Now is a good time for f2-f3. Instead White gets greedy and takes the queen. He'll regret it.

12. gxh4	Nh3#
	0-1

The king is in checkmate.

180. NIMZO-INDIAN

1.	d4	Nf6
2.	c4	e6
3.	Nc3	Bb4
4.	Nf3	0-0
5.	Bf4	Ne4
6.	Rc1	c5
7.	e3	Qf6

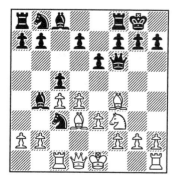

9.	bxc3	Ba3
10.	Bg5	....

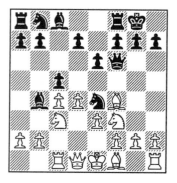

Later the queen gets into trouble so it was probably best to leave her on d8.

8. Bd3   Nxc3

There were two better moves: 8... d5 and 8...cxd4. By trading off on c3, he sets up two White threats.

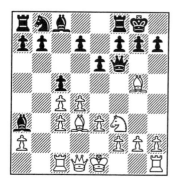

Black saw the threat to his bishop. That why he moved it. He didn't see the threat to trap his queen. That's why he loses it.

181. KING'S INDIAN

1.	d4	Nf6
2.	c4	g6
3.	Nc3	Bg7
4.	e4	d6
5.	f3	0-0
6.	Be3	e5
7.	d5	Ne8

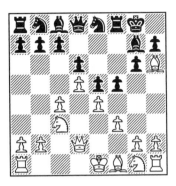

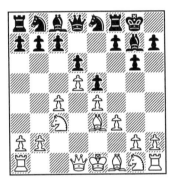

After White closes the center, d5, Black prepares to chip away with ...f5.

8.	Qd2	f5
9.	Bh6	....

White plays a thematic King's Indian move, looking to trade off the g7-bishop. But the move Bh6 comes later on, after White castles queenside. With the king still at e1, it doesn't work.

9.	....	Qh4†
10.	g3	Qxh6

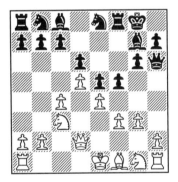

Black wins a bishop for nothing.

182. KING'S INDIAN

1. d4   Nf6
2. c4   g6
3. Nc3   d6
4. Nf3   Nbd7

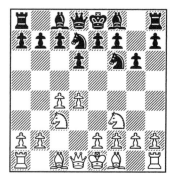

When you start a fianchetto by ...g7-g6, you are supposed to finish it off, ...Bf8-g7. Black can do it now or on his next move. But he'd better do it.

5. Bg5   e5

Black starts new business before he's taken care of old business, ...Bf8-g7. Naturally something bad happens.

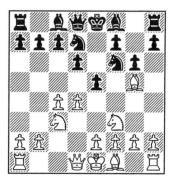

6. dxe5   dxe5
7. Nxe5   Nxe5
8. Qxd8† Kxd8
9. Bxf6† Be7
10. Bxh8 ....

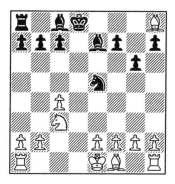

White has come out ahead. He's won a rook.

183. KING'S INDIAN

1.	d4	Nf6
2.	c4	g6
3.	Nc3	Bg7
4.	e4	d6
5.	Nf3	Nbd7
6.	Bg5	c5

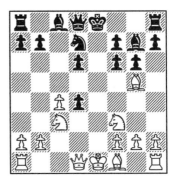

Black figures on getting his piece back.

9. Qxd4 ....

Instead of 6...e5, Black invites complications. Now 7. d5 is safe but White decides to take the plunge.

7. e5   cxd4

Black captures the wrong pawn. He has to take the one at e5.

8. exf6   exf6

But he missed White's ninth move. Now if 9...fxg5, simply 10. Qxg7 leaves White a piece up.

184. KING'S INDIAN

1. **d4**	**Nf6**
2. **c4**	**g6**
3. **Nc3**	**Bg7**
4. **e4**	**d6**
5. **Nf3**	**0-0**
6. **Be2**	**Nbd7**
7. **0-0**	**b6**

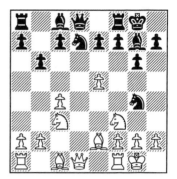

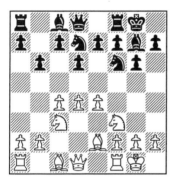

Everything Black did up to this point was fine. But here he had to play 7...e7-e5. That's the way Black fights back in the center in the King's Indian. And if Black doesn't put a pawn on e5, White surely will.

8. **e5**	**dxe5**
9. **dxe5**	**Ng4**

White is just warming up.

10. **e6**	**fxe6**
11. **Ng5**	**Ngf6**
12. **Nxe6**	**Qe8**
13. **Nxc7**	**Qd8**
14. **Nxa8**	**....**

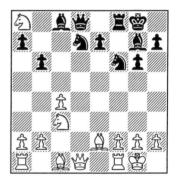

White wins the exchange.

185. GRÜNFELD DEFENSE

1.	d4	Nf6
2.	c4	g6
3.	Nc3	d5
4.	Nf3	Bg7
5.	Bg5	Ne4

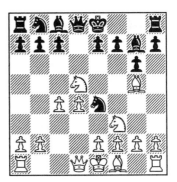

6.	....	Nxg5
7.	Nxg5	e6

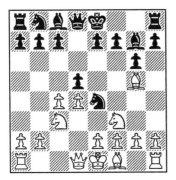

Leaves the d5-pawn in the lurch. White has two ways to capture; one is right the other is wrong.

6. Nxd5 ....

The wrong way to take. When in doubt, take with the lowest value unit. Here it's the pawn, so the correct move was 6. c4xd5.

Both White knights are under attack. White has the choice of which knight he wants to lose. It's not a happy choice.

186. GRÜNFELD DEFENSE

1.	d4	Nf6
2.	c4	g6
3.	g3	d5
4.	e3	Nc6
5.	cxd5	Qxd5
6.	Qf3	Qa5†
7.	Bd2	....

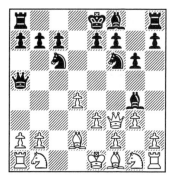

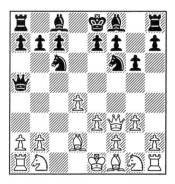

The queen is attacked and should move, 7...Qb6. Instead, Black gets fancy and outsmarts himself.

7.	....	Bg4

Figuring on 9. Bxa5 Bxf3 and then 10. Nxf3 Nxa5, when material is all even. But he hasn't looked at all the captures. White's next knocks the props out from under Black's queen.

9.	Qxc6†	bxc6
10.	Bxa5	....

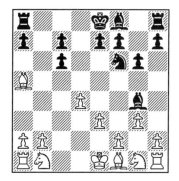

White has won a full knight.

187. GRÜNFELD DEFENSE

1. d4	Nf6
2. c4	g6
3. g3	Bg7
4. Bg2	d5
5. cxd5	Nxd5
6. e4	Nb4
7. Qa4†	....

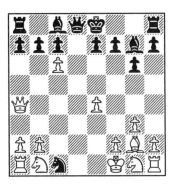

10.	b5
11. Qc2	Bxb2

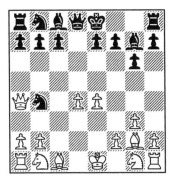

Not as good as it looks; Black has resources. Best play was 7. d4-d5.

7.	N8c6
8. d5	Nd3†
9. Kf1	Nxc1
10. dxc6	....

White may have seen up to here. It's too bad he missed Black's next move.

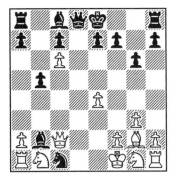

Black wins material. The queen can't take at b2 because of 12... Qd1# The same was true a move earlier, 11. Qxb5? Qd1#.

188. GRÜNFELD DEFENSE

1.	d4	Nf6
2.	c4	g6
3.	Nc3	d5
4.	cxd5	Nxd5
5.	e3	Bg7
6.	Bc4	Nb6
7.	Bb3	c6
8.	Nf3	Nbd7

(A) 10...Kf8 11. Ne6†
(B) 10...Ke8 11. Ne6
(C) 10...Kg8 11. Qb3†

10.	....	Kf6
11.	Nce4†	Kf5
12.	g4#	1-0

Black should have brought his king to safety by castling. Not castling allows White to land a haymaker.

9.	Bxf7†	Kxf7
10.	Ng5†	....

Nothing works.

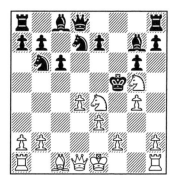

Checkmate with a pawn. I hate getting checkmated by a pawn.

189. GRÜNFELD DEFENSE

1. d4	Nf6
2. c4	g6
3. Nc3	d5
4. cxd5	Nxd5
5. e4	Nxc3
6. bxc3	Bg7

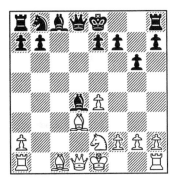

10. Nxd4	Qxd4
11. Bb5†	Nc6
12. Qxd4	....

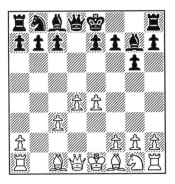

The main line of the Grünfeld. White gets two pawns in the center, but the one at d4 is under fire from the g7-bishop.

7. Bd3	c5
8. Ne2	cxd4
9. cxd4	Bxd4

Black rushes in, thinking he's won a pawn. A much better move was 9...0-0. Then White's center starts to look a bit shaky.

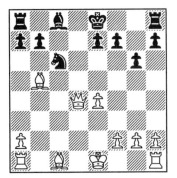

White wins the queen.

TRAP OF THE DAY:
Flank Openings

190. GROB'S ATTACK

1. g4 ....

Henry Grob's invention.

1. .... Nc6
2. e4 Nd4

Better 2...e5. The knight move shouldn't work, but amazingly, it does.

3. Ne2 ....

Better to attack the knight by 3. c3 and after the knight retreats, then 4. d4.

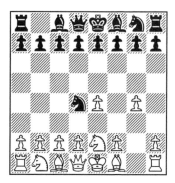

As played, White loses control of f3. Do we need to tell you where the Black knight settles?

3. .... Nf3#
0-1

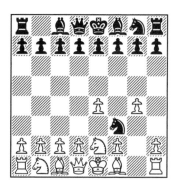

Smothered mate.

191. MIESES OPENING

1.	d3	d5
2.	Bf4	e6
3.	Nd2	Bd6

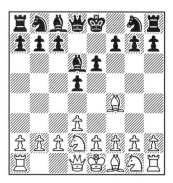

Black develops while attacking the f4-bishop. White has to do something to save his bishop.

4. g3 ....

He should simply exchange on d6. Protecting the bishop with the g-pawn is the wrong thing to do in this situation. You'll see why after Black's next move.

4. .... e5

Attacks the bishop with a pawn. The bishop tries to run, but there's nowhere to hide.

5. Be3 d4

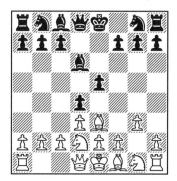

The bishop has become ensnared by the pawns.

192. LARSEN ATTACK

1. b3   e5
2. Ba3   ....

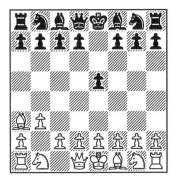

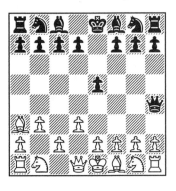

Normally the bishop would go to b2. Maybe White is playing to confuse Black.

2. ....   Qh4

And maybe Black is confused. The queen move is not all that promising.

3. d3   ....

Here he should play 3. Nf3 attacking the queen. Somehow, White has gotten himself confused. That was not supposed to happen.

3. ....   Bxa3
4. Nxa3   Qb4†
5. Qd2   Qxa3

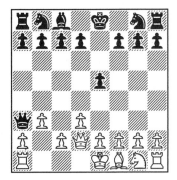

Black ends all the confusion by winning a piece.

193. BENKO OPENING

1.	g3	g6
2.	Bg2	h5
3.	Kf1	....

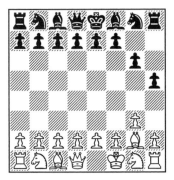

A very weak move. Instead, he should play out his king-knight, 3. Nf3. That would prevent Black from advancing his h-pawn.

3.	....	h4
4.	Nf3	....

Timing is everything in chess. One move earlier this knight move was fine. One move later, it's a mistake. If he had to move the knight, a better square was 4. Nh3.

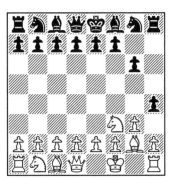

4.	....	h3

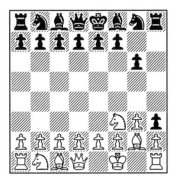

The pawn comes on and traps White's bishop. White could try 5. Bxh3 Rxh3 6. Nh4, trapping Black's rook. But 6...d6 looks to be a sufficient defense.

203

194. BENKO OPENING

1.	g3	e5
2.	Bg2	Nf6
3.	d3	Bc5
4.	Nd2	....

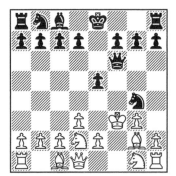

Better first to play 4. Nf3, getting ready to castle.

4.	....	Bxf2†
5.	Kxe2	Ng4†

If 6. Ke1(f1) then 6...Ne3(†) wins the queen. White tries playing the king up but that's even worse.

6.	Kf3	Qf6†

7. Kxg4 ....

If 6. Ke4 Qc6† 8. Kf5 Qg6#.

7.	....	d6†
8.	Kh5	Qh6#

0-1

White has been mated.

195. BIRD OPENING

1.	f4	Nc6
2.	b3	e5
3.	fxe5	Bc5

1. f4   Nc6
2. b3   e5
3. fxe5 Bc5

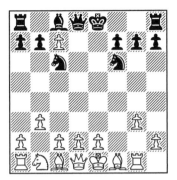

A good developing move was 7. Bb2.

7. ....   Qd4

Black can simply take his pawn back by 3...Nxe5. Instead, he takes a chance, sacrificing pawns to get a jump in development.

4. g3   Bxg1
5. Rxg1   d6
6. exd6   Nf6
7. dxc7   ....

Too greedy. White already has enough pawns. What he needs to do now is get some pieces into the game.

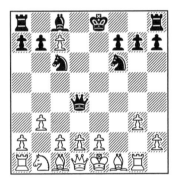

The queen centralizes and forks both rooks. White has to part with one of them. A sad choice.

196. BIRD OPENING

1. f4 ....

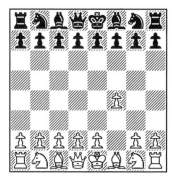

| 2. | .... | Qh4† |
| 3. | g3 | Qxg3# |

0-1

After advancing the f-pawn White has to keep one thing in mind. Any further movement of his other king-side pawns is likely to weaken the diagonal e1-h4.

1. .... e6
2. h3 ....

White does not know the rule or maybe has forgotten it. He could safely play 2. Ng1-f3, but the move played leads to disaster. Now Black gives check which White desperately tries to block.

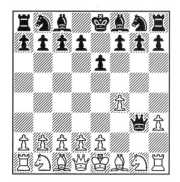

White has been done in along the Fool's Mate diagonal. That will teach him not to move those king-side pawns.

197. BIRD OPENING

1.	f4	Nf6
2.	Nf3	d6

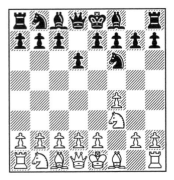

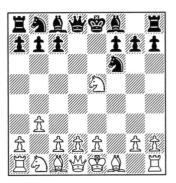

This is a good defense against the Bird. White would like to control the e5-square, but Black, by placing a pawn at d6, makes it hard to do.

3.	b3	e5
4.	fxe5	dxe5
5.	Nxe5	....

This is not a free pawn. White should finish off his fianchetto, 5. Bb2. Then he really does threaten to take on e5.

5. ....   Qd4

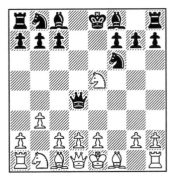

Forking knight and rook, winning one of them. We've examined 6. Nc4 Qxa1 7. Bb2 Qxa2 8. Nc3, but the queen escapes by 8...Qa6. So this line doesn't work for White.

198. RETI OPENING

1.	Nf3	b6
2.	b4	Bb7
3.	Bb2	Bxf3
4.	gxf3	a5
5.	a3	axb4
6.	axb4	Rxa1
7.	Bxa1	Nf6
8.	e3	d6
9.	Bb5†	Nbd7

White has a good game and can take control of the long diagonal by 10. Bc6. This is excellent preparation for his next move.

10. f4 ....

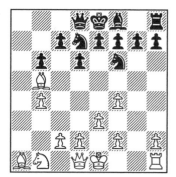

To control e5. In principal this is a fine idea, but here it is premature and fails for tactical reasons.

10. .... Qa8

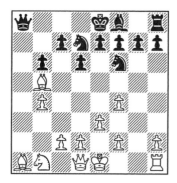

Forking the White pieces in the corners, Ba1 and Rh1.

208

199. RETI OPENING

1. Nf3	Nc6
2. g3	e5
3. d3	d5
4. Nbd2	f6
5. Bg2	Be6
6. e4	dxe4
7. dxe4	Qd7
8. 0-0	....

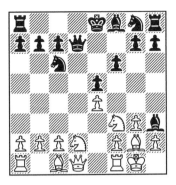

9. Nxe5	Nxe5
10. Qh5†	g6
11. Qxh3	....

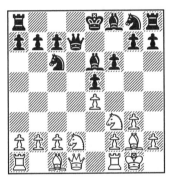

A Pirc Defense with colors reversed. That means White is playing a Black defense but with an extra move thrown in.

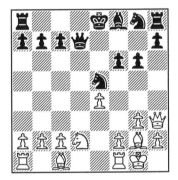

White wins an important center pawn.

8. .... Bh3

He should first castle on the queenside. The bishop move doesn't work with the Black king still standing on his starting square.

200. RETI OPENING

1.	Nf3	d5
2.	g3	Nf6
3.	Bg2	Bf5
4.	c4	e6
5.	cxd5	exd5
6.	Qb3	Nbd7

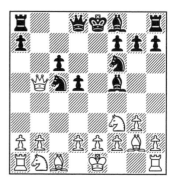

Indirect defense of the b7-pawn. But White figures he can snap off the pawn and still get his queen out. He's mistaken.

7.	Qxb7	....

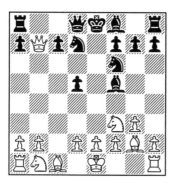

7.	....	Nc5
8.	Qb5†	c6

Blocks the check. If the queen takes at c6, then 9...Bd7 traps the queen.

9.	Qb4	....

He tries another square.

9.	....	Nd3†

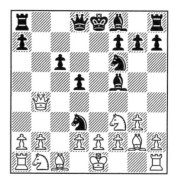

10...Bxb4 wins the queen.

201. ENGLISH OPENING

1.	c4	Nc6
2.	e3	d6
3.	Ne2	Ne5

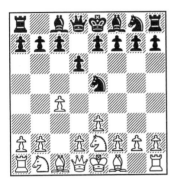

The knight moves into the center and makes two threats. Sadly, White sees only one of the threats.

4. f4 ....

White thinks he's setting a trap for his opponent. What he's really doing is setting a trap for himself. The right move was 4. d4, chasing the enemy knight back. As for Black, he originally thought he could take 4...Nxc4, but then he noticed White's trick, 5. Qa4† forking king and knight. Looking around, he then found a better move.

4. .... Nd3#
0-1

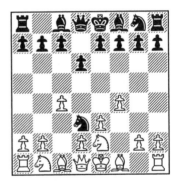

Smothered mate by the knight.

202. ENGLISH OPENING

1.	c4	c5
2.	Nf3	Nf6
3.	Nc3	g6
4.	d3	b6
5.	Bd2	e6

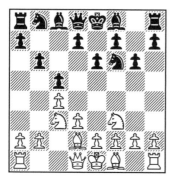

Black has started to flank both his bishops (...g6 and ...b6) but has yet to finish off what he started. This was a good moment to do it, 5... Bc8-b7. It would prevent White's next move.

6. Ne4   Bb7

Now this comes one move too late. Best was to take, 6...Nxe4.

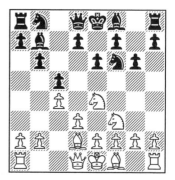

7.	Nxf6†	Qxf6
8.	Bc3	....

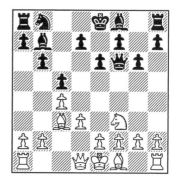

White has fashioned a skewer on the long dark-squared diagonal. After the queen moves off, say 8... Qd8, White takes the rook in the corner, 9. Bxh8.

203. ENGLISH OPENING

1.	c4	c6
2.	Nc3	d5
3.	e3	Nf6
4.	cxd5	cxd5
5.	Bb5†	Bd7
6.	Nge2	a6
7.	Bxd7†	Qxd7
8.	b4	e5
9.	Rb1	b5

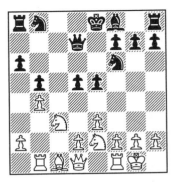

10.	....	d4
11.	exd4	exd4

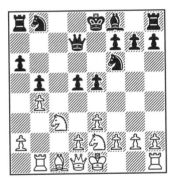

Contains a threat which White overlooks.

10. 0-0 ....

Careless castling which shows that White is not looking at the board. This was a good moment for the advance of the d2-pawn, either 10. d3 or 10. d4.

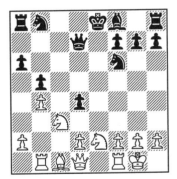

White loses a piece as the knight at c3 has no safe escape square.

204. ENGLISH OPENING

1. c4	e6
2. g3	Bb4

This move would make sense if White had played 2. Nc3. Then the bishop might "threaten" to take the knight. Actually it's not that big a threat. But there's no knight on c3, so it's hard to figure out what the bishop is doing on b4. Pinning the d2-pawn?

3. a3	Ba5

White shoos away the bishop and the bishop moves off in the wrong direction. The proper play was to retreat along the a3-f8 diagonal.

4. b4	Bb6
5. c5	....

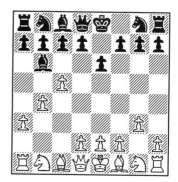

One Black bishop trapped and lost to the advancing White pawns.

205. ENGLISH OPENING

1.	c4	e5
2.	d4	d6

Guards e5. Simpler and better is to exchange, 2...exd4 3. Qxd4 Nc6.

3.	dxe5	dxe5
4.	Qxd8†	Kxd8
5.	a3	Be7
6.	Nf3	e4
7.	Ne5	Nh6

8.	Bxh6	gxh6
9.	Nxf7†	Ke8
10.	Nxh8	....

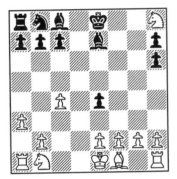

Black has been coping up to this point and here he should guard f7 with his king, 7...Ke8. Protection by the knight is an illusion, quickly dispelled.

The knight will not likely get out of the corner, but no matter. White has won the exchange.

206. ENGLISH OPENING

1.	c4	e5
2.	e3	d5
3.	cxd5	Qxd5
4.	Ne2	....

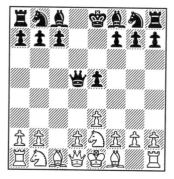

More natural is 4. Nc3, attacking the queen directly. White comes to this idea on the next move.

4.	....	Bg4
5.	Nec3	....

Now Black figures it's a case of "I take your queen, you take my queen. Even trade." It's not as simple as that. Instead, Black should back off, 5...Qd7.

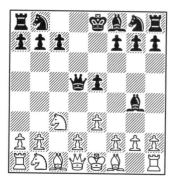

5.	....	Bxd1
6.	Nxd5	....

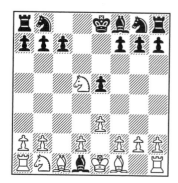

At the end White has a double threat: 7. Nxc7† and 7. Kxd1. There's no way for Black to meet both threats at once, so White wins material.

207. ENGLISH OPENING

1.	c4	e5
2.	g3	Bb4

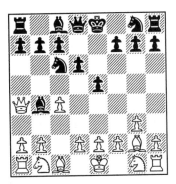

The bishop waits for a knight to turn up at c3, when he intends to take, ...Bxc3. But if no knight comes to c3, the bishop just gets into trouble.

3. Bg2   d6

That's it; bishop in trouble. The better line of play was 3...Nf6 followed by 5...0-0.

4. Qa4†   Nc6

Black tries to protect both his king and his b4-bishop.

It can't be done because White can knock out the knight—which he does.

5.	Bxc6†	bxc6
6.	Qxb4	....

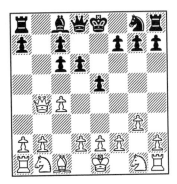

White comes away with a free bishop.

208. ENGLISH OPENING

1.	c4	e5
2.	Nf3	Bd6

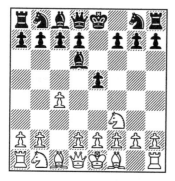

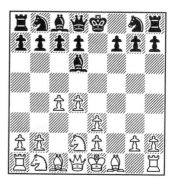

5.	....	Qh4†
6.	g3	Bxg3†
7.	hxg3	Qxg3#
	0-1	

Blocking the d7-pawn can't be recommended. However, as this game shows, even a second-rate move cannot be underestimated.

3.	d4	e4
4.	Nfd2	e3
5.	fxe3	....

After 5. Nf3 exf2+ 6. Kxf2, White is inconvenienced by having moved his king, but nothing terrible is going to happen. However, grabbing the pawn proves fatal.

Another version of the Fool's Mate.

209. ENGLISH OPENING

1.	c4	e5
2.	Nf3	Nc6
3.	g3	Nd4
4.	Nxe5	....

White asks for trouble. Both 4. Nxd4 and 4. Bg2 were good replies.

4.	....	Qe7

Lining up against the knight and indirectly against the White king.

5. Nd3 ....

The only defense was 5. f4 d6 6. e3 dxe5 7. exd4. At the end of the sequence Black recovers his pawn, 7...exd4† or 7...exf4†, with the superior position.

5.	....	Nf3#
	0-1	

A smothered pin mate.

210. ENGLISH OPENING

1.	c4	e5
2.	d3	d6
3.	Nf3	Nc6
4.	g3	Be6
5.	Bg2	Qd7
6.	0-0	0-0-0
7.	Qa4	Kb8
8.	Rd1	Bh3
9.	Bh1	....

10. Qxd7 Nxe2#
0-1

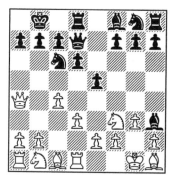

To preserve the bishop and protect his king. In fact he puts his king in danger. Correct was 9. Nc3.

9. .... Nd4

Threats to both the king and queen. White sees the one but misses the other. But even if he saves his king he would still lose his queen.

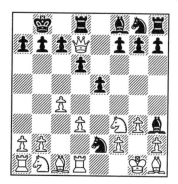

White has been mated.

220

211. ENGLISH OPENING

1. c4	e5
2. d3	Bc5
3. Nf3	d6
4. g3	f5
5. Bg2	e4
6. Ng5	....

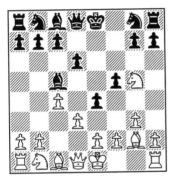

Safer 6. dxe4 fxe4 7. Nd4, centralizing the knight.

6.	e3
7. Bxe3	....

White's attention is focused on the pawn that just moved to e3. He doesn't see beyond the pawn to his knight at g5. If he had, he might play 7. Nh3 or 7. f4, when everything is covered.

7.	Bxe3
8. fxe3	Qxg5

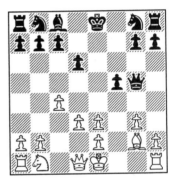

Knocking out the defending bishop, Black walks off with an extra knight.

212. ENGLISH OPENING

1.	c4	e5
2.	d3	Nf6
3.	Nf3	....

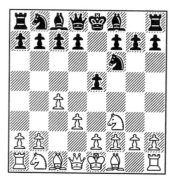

Attacking a pawn. Black is supposed to do something about it, like defend it.

3.	....	c6

Maybe Black doesn't see it. If you believe that, you're just as gullible as White is.

4.	Nxe5	....

Of course, Black defended his pawn. But he did it indirectly, setting a trap.

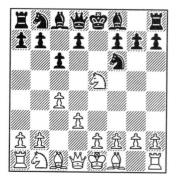

White just didn't see it.

4.	....	Qa5†
5.	Nc3	Qxe5

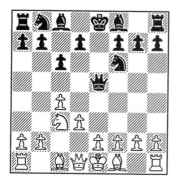

White has an extra pawn; Black has an extra knight. We like the extra knight.

213. ENGLISH OPENING

1.	c4	e5
2.	Nc3	c6

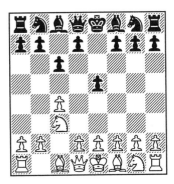

Intending ...d7-d5, placing two pawns in the center. White should take this last move as a signal to start an attack on the e5-pawn: 3. d4 or 3. Nf3. He doesn't.

3.	g3	d5
4.	cxd5	cxd5
5.	Bg2	d4
6.	Ne4	....

White has done nothing to hold back Black's pawns. As a result the knight is driven from its post.

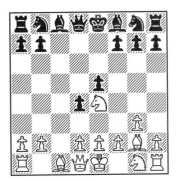

Safest was the knight back to b1.

6.	....	f5

The knight is caught in mid-board, surrounded by Black pawns. With no way out White loses a knight.

214. ENGLISH OPENING

1.	c4	e5
2.	Nc3	c6
3.	g3	d5
4.	cxd5	cxd5
5.	d4	exd4
6.	Qxd4	Nf6
7.	Bg5	Be7

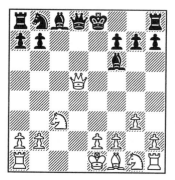

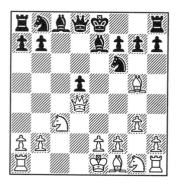

White has done a good job of fighting for the center, but here he overrates his position. He needs to bring out more pieces, so 8. Bg2 is likely the right move.

8.	Bxg5	Bxf6
9.	Qxd5	....

Black's d-pawn was not so weak that it could be taken by force. White discovers this too late. He should have moved his queen.

9.	....	Bxc3†
10.	bxc3	Qxd5

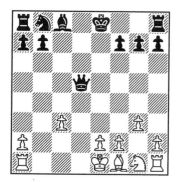

Black wins the queen.

215. ENGLISH OPENING

1.	c4	e5
2.	Nc3	Nc6
3.	d3	d6
4.	Nf3	Be6
5.	Qa4	Qd7
6.	Nd5	....

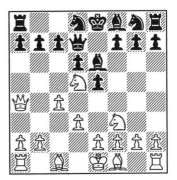

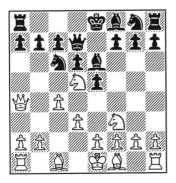

7.	Nxc7†	Ke7
8.	Qxd7†	Kxd7
9.	Nxa8	....

One of White's main ideas in the English is to get control of d5. He's managed to do that here, and Black has to find a way to deal with the annoying d5-knight.

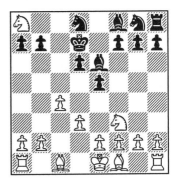

Black is minus one rook.

6.	....	Nd8

Planning to oust the knight by ...c7-c6. It doesn't work, so he just has to live with it. 6...Be7, 7...Nf6, and 8...0-0 was the way to go.

216. ENGLISH OPENING

1. c4   e5
2. Nc3   Nf6
3. Nf3   Nc6
4. g3   d5
5. cxd5   Nxd5
6. Bg2   ....

Aiming at the d5-knight. A discovery is in the air.

6. ....   Be7

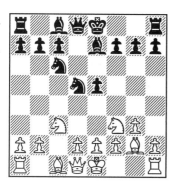

Black doesn't see what's coming. The knight had to back off, 6... Nd5-b6.

7. Nxe5   ....

If 7...Nxe5 then 8. Nxd5. Black varies to change the course of events.

7. ....   Nxc3
8. Bxc6†   bxc6
9. dxc3   ....

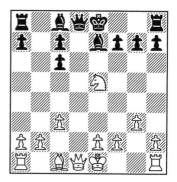

White has won an important center pawn.

217. JOKE OPENING

1. h3   ....

Psychology. White plays a series of beginner moves to lull his opponent into a false sense of security.

1.	....	e5
2.	e4	Bc5
3.	Bc4	Nf6
4.	Qf3	0-0
5.	g4	c6

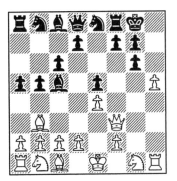

Now 10...g5 is in order.

10.	....	a4
11.	hxg6	axb3

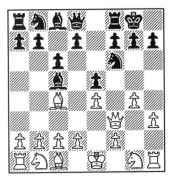

6.	g5	Ne8
7.	h4	b5
8.	Bb3	a5
9.	g6	hxg6
10.	h5	....

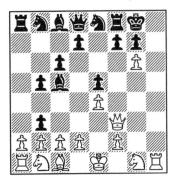

Checkmate in three moves: 12. Rh8† Kxh8 13. Qh5† Kg8 14. Qh7# 1-0. Moral: even a bogus opening has to be taken seriously.

OPENING INDEX

DOUBLE KING PAWN OPENINGS

 **TACTICAL INDEX**

Numbers on this page refer to Opening Trap # (not page #).